BURKE HEDG

# You Can't Steal Second With Your Foot On First!

*The most valuable 100 people to bring into a deteriorating society would not be 100 chemists, or politicians, or professors, or engineers. But rather 100 entrepreneurs.*
— Abraham H. Maslow

**You Can't Steal Second With Your Foot On First!**
By Burke Hedges

Printed in the United States of America
First Edition, August 1995

ISBN 0-9632667-1-3

Published by INTI Publishing
Tampa, FL
(813) 881-1638

Book design by Cherry Design

# DEDICATION

To all the *dissatisfied employees* who ever dreamed of going into business for themselves — and then had the courage to do something about it.

# CONTENTS

# Contents

# ACKNOWLEDGMENT

There are two business axioms I never waiver from: One, the only boss you should ever answer to is yourself. And two, surround yourself with good people and give them the freedom and encouragement to do what they do best.

I can think of no better place than a book about free enterprise to acknowledge the talented people whom I'm fortunate to work with.

A special acknowledgment and deep gratitude goes to Dr. Stephen W. Price — my partner, advisor and friend — for his invaluable contributions to this book and to my various business endeavors.

My love and gratitude to Sandee Lorenzen, INTI Director of Operations, for her great attitude and awesome efficiency. *Sandee, you're tops!*

Many thanks to Jewel Parago, our bookkeeper extraordinaire and financial strategist, for her sage advice and daily diligence. *Jewel, you're amazing!*

My sincere respect and admiration to Mike Boyer, my partner in Equibore of America, for his commitment and vision. *Mike, you're the best!*

My deepest respect and appreciation to Sandra Bailey, my personal assistant at Equibore of America, for her infinite patience and undying dedication. *Sandra, you're wonderful!*

Last but not least, all my love and devotion to my wife Debbie and our four beautiful children — Burke, Nathen, Spencer and Aspen — for giving me the support and freedom I need to pursue my entrepreneurial dreams. *Debbie and the kids, you're my everything!*

# The High Price Of Dependence

*You are free the moment you stop looking outside yourself for someone to solve your problems.*
— H. Jackson Brown, Jr.

You'll never fully appreciate what the word "free" in free enterprise means until it has been taken from you.

I know, because in 1959 my father was a successful businessman in Cuba worth over $20 million. When Fidel Castro and his communist government took over the country, my parents were forced to escape overnight with just the clothes on their backs.

I tell you this because I see millions of my fellow Americans taking free enterprise for granted! And it breaks my heart!

The sad truth is, Americans have conditioned themselves to believe in a movement almost as dangerous as *Communism*. I call it *Job-ism*.

Under *Communism*, the government takes away your freedom and forces you to depend on them for all your basic needs.

1

Under *Job-ism*, you voluntarily give away your freedom in exchange for a weekly paycheck.

That's why I decided to write this book.

To warn you to *beware of the velvet trap of job-dependence.*

To let you know *there's a high price to be paid for depending on the government or an employer for your livelihood.*

To steer you back on the right path, once and for all, to *independence through free enterprise!*

## What You Can Expect From This Book

In the first section of this book, titled "Either Way, You Pay!" you'll learn that the key to independence has been right in front of you all along. You'll learn that the price you'll pay for a life of mediocrity is much higher than the price you'll have to pay for success.

In the second section, titled "An American Addiction — Being Broke," you'll learn why being broke is reaching epidemic proportions and why there's a big difference between being broke and being poor. Finally, you'll learn about the myth of job-security and why jobs are becoming less and less secure.

In the final section, "An Intelligent Alternative: Independence Through Free Enterprise," you'll learn the secret of creating — and keeping — wealth. You'll learn about what I consider to be the ideal business for the coming decade, and you'll be challenged to break out of the cycle of dependence once and for all by signing your personal Declaration of Independence!

I'd like to think this book is more than a book about making money or going into business for yourself. It's really about making choices. Here's a poem that says it better than I ever could:

*There was a very cautious man*
*Who never laughed or played.*
*He never risked, he never tried;*
*He never sang or prayed.*
*And when he one day passed away*
*His insurance was denied.*
*For since he never lived,*
*They claimed he never died.*
— Anonymous

It's my sincere hope that this book will encourage you to choose independence over dependence...to free yourself from a boss...to choose to act rather than procrastinate...and to choose, above all, to live your life with purpose and passion rather than fearful caution.

# PART 1

# Either Way, You Pay!

# 1

# The Day I Won $86 Million!

*A little government and a little luck are necessary in life,*
*but only a fool trusts either of them.*

*— P. J. O'Rourke*

I'LL NEVER FORGET THE DAY I HELD THE WIN-
NING NUMBERS worth $86 million in the Florida
lottery! In fact, I remember everything about the day
so clearly it seems like only yesterday.

It was Saturday, March 20, 1993. No one had
picked the winning numbers the previous three or
four weeks, so the jackpot kept growing and growing
— until it hit $86 million! All week long people
lined up in gas stations and convenience stores waiting to buy their tickets. Everywhere you went people
were joking about what they'd do with the money
when they hit the $86 million jackpot.

I was in Orlando that day conducting a seminar.
My wife Debbie drove up from our home in St.
Petersburg to join me for the evening. On her way,
she stopped for gas at a convenience store and pur-
chased three lottery tickets.

The next day we drove back to our home, where we were entertaining some friends for dinner. When we arrived home Debbie casually placed the lottery tickets next to the Sunday paper on the kitchen counter. I couldn't help but notice the winning numbers splashed across the front page.

As everybody watched, I checked the three tickets against the winning numbers for the week. The first ticket was a bust. Only two numbers matched. The second ticket was even worse. No numbers matched!

"Same old, same old," I remarked to our dinner guests, who were gathered around watching. As I checked the third ticket against the winning numbers, I could feel the hair starting to raise on the back of my neck...7-14-18-47-12-27. I stared at the newspaper. I glanced back at my ticket. 7-14-18-47-12-27. My pulse quickened.

Was I imagining things, or did our numbers match the winning numbers listed in the newspaper? I glanced back at the newspaper, then the ticket. Back to the newspaper. Back to the ticket.

Each time I checked my lottery ticket, my pulse increased...my breathing got shallower...more rapid. My hands were literally trembling now.

Finally, I read the numbers from the newspaper slowly aloud as I checked them against our ticket. I even read them backwards, just to be extra sure.

They matched! THEY MATCHED!

"WE WON THE LOTTERY," I screamed, as I leaped from my chair. "WE WON $86 MILLION DOLLARS. WE'RE RICH! WE WON! WE WON!", I screamed as I jumped around the room like a human pogo stick. Can you imagine how I felt?

After a few moments I realized something was wrong. It didn't take me long to notice I was the only one celebrating.

My wife, of all things, was laughing.

My best friend, Jake, was pounding the wall, laughing hysterically.

My wife, between fits of laughter, explained that she'd pulled into the gas station *after* the drawing, which was held every Saturday evening. The winning numbers had already been posted in the store. So she decided to play a practical joke on me. She bought a lottery ticket for the next week's lottery with the same numbers as the winning ticket worth $86 million.

I'd been had. It was time for a reality check.

## Reality Check

Talk about embarrassed! I flopped down in my chair, feeling like a total idiot.

I fell for a great practical joke...hook, line and sinker.

But as the laughter of my friends echoed around me, I felt a sudden sense of relief. I realized how special this moment was. I'd just felt something that very few people in the world have ever felt.

"Hold on a minute...hold on," I shouted with a mock seriousness. "There's something I want to say to all of you."

The room got very quiet. "I want you to realize," I said, "that I'm the only one in this room who knows what it really feels like to win $86 million dollars.

And I wanna tell ya, IT FELT GREAT!"

From the back of the room a single voice replied, "You're also the only one who knows what it FEELS LIKE TO LOSE $86 MILLION, TOO! "

And we all cracked up with laughter.

## The Lottery Mentality

I'm telling you this story because I see so many talented, able-bodied Americans falling for what I call the "quick-fix-lottery mentality." These wishful thinkers are *counting on the lottery* to finance their dreams.

Right...and I've got a bridge in Brooklyn to sell you.

Look, you've literally got a better chance of being struck by lightning than winning the lottery. Check this out: In 1993, almost 14 million people played the weekly Florida lottery. Know how many won?...45! Forty-five winners and *13,714,855 losers. How's that for odds?!!*

Hey, don't get me wrong. I'm not necessarily knocking lotteries. I still buy a ticket or two whenever I happen to be in a convenience store. You'll never win if you don't play, right? And to me, the *entertainment value* of playing the lottery is worth a buck or two a month.

On the other hand, playing the lottery is in no way a legitimate strategy for achieving financial independence!

## The Job Mentality

I see these same talented, able-bodied Americans clinging to an out-dated belief system that's as bogus as the lottery mentality. I call it the "gotta-get-a-good-job" mentality. These people are counting on their jobs to provide them with a substantial income and a secure future.

Just more wishful thinking.

Like people with the lottery mentality, most employees are chasing a carrot their employers will never let them have — annual raises and cradle-to-grave employment. Statistics show that the typical American worker will have 10 to 12 different jobs in four to five different career areas. Where's the security in that?

Right goal, wrong strategy, friend. Here's the plain, unvarnished truth:

*If you're depending on your job or on winning the lottery to achieve financial independence, you're the butt of a huge practical joke, bigger than the one my wife played on me!*

Sadly, we're becoming a nation of wishful thinkers, hoping to win the lottery...crossing our fingers that we won't lose our job in the next round of layoffs. Seems like we're being played for suckers 'cause the only ones really getting ahead are the ones selling the dreams!

As the old poker-playing adage goes, "If you're invited to play poker, be sure to look around the table and spot the sucker before you sit down to play. If you don't see one, get up and leave—'cause you're the sucker!"

## Don't Fall For Wishful Thinking

Listen, friend, don't be a sucker...don't confuse the *entertainment* derived from playing the lottery — and the *temporary income* derived from your job — with real *opportunities* available through the free enterprise system!

The only way you can achieve independence is to exchange your wishful thinking for purposeful action! Which means you're going to have to make a tough decision to step out of your comfort zone...take a calculated risk...and go for it!

# 2

# To Live Is To Risk

*There's no getting away from risks. There's only recognizing them, managing them, and deciding which ones you can take.*

— Lynn Hopewell

SHOCK
ANGER.
SADNESS.
LOVE.

Those are just a few of the emotions I felt in the aftermath of the bombing of the Oklahoma City federal building.

Shock that someone would bomb a building...in Oklahoma City, of all places. Anger at the cowardly perpetrators. Sadness for the families who lost loved ones, especially children. And love for my wife and four children.

The Oklahoma City tragedy just serves to remind us how vulnerable we are...and how we can't take a day, not even a moment, for granted because it may be our last.

## You Can't Get Away From Risk

We live in dangerous times, no question about it. I mean, if you're not safe in a U.S. federal building, then you're not safe anywhere, are you? As the old saying goes…"there are no guarantees in this life."

Let's face it. To live is to risk. You can't get away from it.

To love is to risk getting your heart broken.

To marry is to risk getting divorced.

To breathe is to risk getting poisoned by air pollution.

To settle for a "secure" job is to risk getting laid off.

We live in the real world, not Fantasy Island, and we've got to deal with it.

## Managing Risk

True, you can't avoid risk. But to some degree, you can manage it.

Physicians, for example, say people are "at-risk" if they consume high-fat diets, don't exercise, smoke cigarettes and are heavy drinkers. All the studies prove at-risk people have higher incidences of cancer and heart disease.

Now, most people would call me a risk-taker. And compared to the average Joe, I see why someone would say that.

I started nine different businesses before my 31st birthday. I've scuba dived, bungee jumped, and invested hundreds of thousands of dollars of my own cash in business endeavors that turned sour. And yes, I admit to getting a speeding ticket or two over the years. But in each of those situations, I didn't consider my behavior risky 'cause *I was in control of each situation.*

I did my homework...I knew the risk. And with the possible exception of bungee jumping, I was in charge the whole time.

I get a kick out of people when they tell me they don't want to go into business for themselves because it's *too risky.* I say to them, "That's odd. That's why I'll never work for someone else as long as I live — it's too risky!"

Think about it...Would you let someone else raise your kids? Would you let someone other than your spouse have access to your checking and savings accounts? Of course not!

And why not? 'Cause it's too risky, that's why! You'd be volunteering to give up control to someone else, leaving yourself wide open to be used and abused. No sane, thinking adult would ever do that, would they?

So why would you volunteer to give an employer total control over your personal finances, your mortgage, your car payment, your kid's college fund and your health insurance in exchange for a monthly paycheck? Does this make good sense? Of course not!

Think about it...if you're employed, the only two words between you and the street are, "You're fired!" You call that security? I call that *the ultimate in risky business!*

## How To Evaluate A Risk

Years ago I read an interview with Norman Lear, creator of the classic TV series *All in the Family*. Lear was talking about his career as a writer and producer, and he mentioned how important it was to take personal and professional risks.

He said something I've thought about hundreds of times since. "When you're deciding whether or not to take a risk," he said, "ask yourself two questions: One, what was the worst thing that could realistically happen if you failed? And two, if the worst happened, could you live with it?"

Every time I've started a new venture or invested in a new business, I ask myself those two questions before signing on the dotted line.

Now, I want you to know I don't take risk lightly. Besides myself, I have my wife and four lovely children to consider, so I'm anything but a compulsive risk-taker or gambler. And believe me, there's a **BIG** difference between taking a risk and taking a gamble. I know 'cause I've done a lot of the former and a little of the latter. Here are a couple of examples that will illustrate the difference between gambling and calculated risk-taking.

Let's say you had $1,000 to invest. If you went to Vegas and plopped down all of it on red at the roulette table, you could double your money with one spin of the wheel. But you'd have more than an even chance you'd lose it all! That's gambling!

On the other hand, if you invested that same

$1,000 in a couple of proven blue chip stocks, like Coca-Cola International, you'd stand a very good chance of making 10 percent or more on your long-term investment without jeopardizing the principle.

Sure, your stock could go down in the short run. But you'd be taking a *calculated risk* that your blue chip stock would perform well in the future based on its past. In the worst-case scenario, you'd always have something to show for your money.

The big difference between taking a gamble (THE LOTTERY MENTALITY) and taking a calculated risk is what I call the "You Factor," which means *YOU are in control.* When you gamble, *you have very little say* in the outcome. When you invest in stocks, however, if you don't like what your broker is doing, *you can always sell your shares and cash out.*

The bigger the bucks, the more important the "you factor." That's why venture capitalists want to own 70–80–90 percent of a company. They put up the money, they want control over how it's spent.

Two key words here, folks. *You control.* In short, calculated risk-taking is much wiser and more conservative than reckless gambling.

## Either Way, You Pay!

Look, I understand why so many people are reluctant to take risks. In a word, they're afraid of failure.

What would the neighbors say *if I failed?*

How would I replace my savings *if I failed?*

How could I start over at my age *if I failed?*

Sound familiar?

17

Granted, these are all legitimate concerns. But ask yourself this question: "Do you think successful people have the same fears as you?" You bet they do! The difference is they have learned to weigh those fears against the potential return...and they overcome their fears through action.

Check this out: *USA Today* reports that founders of 328 fast-growing businesses risked an average of $82,300 to start their companies. Where did the money come from? Savings, family and friends, that's where.

If they succeed, they pay with long hours and tough decisions — but they receive tremendous rewards! If they fail, they pay by losing their hard-earned money, a loss of confidence and a bruised ego. If they do nothing, they pay by living a life of mediocrity. That's what I mean when I say, "Either way, you pay!"

I don't know about you, but I'll pay the price of success over failure any ol' day!

One thing's for sure. I don't want to be like the character John in the Garfield cartoon where John says, "Garfield, I wonder if I've lived any former lives."

Garfield gives him a scornful look and says, "I doubt it. You're not even living this one."

Hey, I don't pretend to know the full meaning of life. But I do know what it's NOT. Life is NOT a dress rehearsal. And it sure as heck is NOT a spectator sport. I don't know about you, but I'd hate to die knowing that I went to battle against fear and surrendered without a fight. After all, wouldn't you rather be playing in the game than sitting on the bench watching?

## Justification: The Enemy Within

Have you ever noticed how people justify their shortcomings? If they're 50 pounds overweight, they say, "Hey, it could be worse. I could be 100 pounds overweight. Compared to John, I'm skinny!"

Ever think about what we're really doing when we justify, say, working at a job we hate? When we justify, we're trying to convince ourselves that it's OK to settle for second best...that it's OK to play it safe...that it's OK to sell yourself short.

IT'S NOT OK! ...AND YOU KNOW IT!

IT'S NOT OK to have the ability to run a successful business you'd enjoy but to settle for a job because you don't have the courage to take a calculated risk and start your own business.

Abraham Maslow, the world-famous psychologist, said it best: "Anyone who sets out to be less than he is capable of will be unhappy for the rest of his life."

Now, notice that Maslow didn't say happy people had more money...or won more awards. Just look at Elvis Presley, Marilyn Monroe and Jimi Hendricks, to name a few. These people proved that money alone can't buy happiness. What Maslow said was that "self-actualized" people work toward realizing their fullest potential.

In other words, happy, fulfilled people don't justify why they don't have this or that. They tuck their excuses in their back pocket and just go for it!

## If At First You Don't Succeed, Change Your Approach

This country is so concerned with winning that we've developed a pathological fear of failure. Truth is, failure isn't so bad. Truth is, failure is necessary. Failure can be good for you.

Personally, I know what it feels like to fail because I've had several businesses go south. Yet I've always, *always* learned valuable lessons from my failures, lessons that I never would have learned if I hadn't failed. Turns out that these lessons were essential to the success of future businesses.

Now, some of you reading this book may be struggling in a business of your own. Having been there myself, I know what you're going through. My advice to you is to hang in there. Stay in the game. Independence is a long-term proposition, not a quick fix. Approach your business as if you were running a marathon, not a 100-yard dash! If you don't like the results you're getting right now, change your approach. But never, ever give up on free enterprise!

There's no shame in having a business fail. The only shame is repeating the same mistake in your next business. Or worse, giving up on your dream all together because of a setback or two.

Woody Allen once remarked that "The audience is always right." Free enterprise is always right, too. If you have a failing business, it's not the fault of free enterprise. Like I said, you may have to change your approach. You may even have to change your

20

business. But never change your mind about owning your own business!

## You Stumble Only If You're Moving

Remember the New Coke fiasco several years back? It was probably the most disastrous product launch since the Edsel. Maybe the biggest of all time. The marketing guy who engineered the New Coke strategy, Sergio Zyman, resigned in disgrace over the failed campaign. He kicked around as a consultant for seven years before he was offered another job.

Know who hired him? Ready? Coca-Cola, his former employer, that's who!

Here's what the president of Coke, Roberto Goizueta, said about his decision to hire the man responsible for the New Coke disaster.

*We become uncompetitive by not being tolerant of mistakes. The moment you let avoiding failure become your motivator, you're down the path of inactivity. You can stumble only if you're moving.*

Now think about it! If the president of Coca-Cola International encourages his employees to take risks — with literally billions and billions of dollars at stake — who are you and I to play it safe? I believe that if you don't have much, that's the best time to take a risk because you have so little to lose! Whatever you do, don't get discouraged.

History is littered with heroes who failed. Walt Disney was once fired from a job for a "singular lack of drawing ability." Both Disney and Henry Ford went bankrupt with early ventures before becoming household names.

How do you think they felt at that very moment of bankruptcy? I'm sure they were devastated! They didn't have a crystal ball that said they'd hit the jackpot on the next deal. Let's face it, great successes have moments of great failure. Like you and me, legends like Ford and Disney were not immune to failure.

They had moments of doubt and despair. They had moments of disappointment and depression. But they treated failure as a temporary setback, not a life sentence. And that made all the difference!

Hey, I don't know if you have what it takes to become the next Henry Ford. You may not even have what it takes to keep the doors open, much less go down in history.

But one thing I know for sure. And you can etch this in stone:

You'll never know unless you try.

# 3

## Change...Or Be Changed!

*Keep your mind open to change at all times.*
*Welcome it. Court it.*
— *Dale Carnegie*

One of my business partners, Dr. Steve Price, used
to be a high school English teacher. One day we
were talking about the sorry state of education, and I
made the remark that kids weren't motivated to learn
anymore.

"Ever wonder why they aren't more motivated?" he
asked. "Think back to your days in school. How
many intelligent, dedicated, passionate teachers did
you have during high school? Two...maybe three, if
you were lucky."

"Problem is," he continued, "the teaching profes-
sion is filled with what I call 'Matts.' Matts are dull,
predictable people frozen in their comfort
zones...and they're drawn to teaching like bees to
honey because they think it's the most secure job in
the world."

Then he told me the story about Matt.

23

## Zoned Out In His Comfort Zone

*When I was teaching, I ate lunch at the same time in the same place with the same teachers, day in and day out, for over 10 years. I'll never forget this one math teacher named Matt. No matter what was on the menu, Matt ordered the same thing for lunch every day, a plain peanut butter sandwich on white bread.*

*One day I made it a point to sit next to Matt during lunch. I was dying to know why he ordered the same thing for lunch every single day.*

*"So Matt," I said casually, "I see you're having a peanut butter sandwich again today, just like every day. Man, you must really like peanut butter, huh?"*

*"Not really," replied Matt.*

*"Oh, then you must eat it for the protein. Peanut butter is full of protein," I said.*

*"Never really thought about it," replied Matt.*

*"Ah-h-h, I know. You're on a budget, right? Pretty cheap lunch, peanut butter."*

*"Nope. Soup's cheaper," replied Matt.*

*I could feel my voice rising as I said, "Look, Matt, you've ordered a peanut butter sandwich every single day for 10 years. You aren't crazy about the taste. You don't eat it for the nutritional value. And you can afford to order just about anything you want. Let me ask you just one more question.*

*"SO WHY DO YOU ORDER A PEANUT BUTTER SANDWICH EVERY SINGLE DAY OF YOUR LIFE?!!!" I screamed.*

*Startled, Matt placed his sandwich gently on his plate,*

*glanced down at the floor and then said, "Because that's what I've always ordered." With that he returned to his sandwich and the conversation ended.*

## Breaking Out

Now, I've never met Matt personally. But I must say I've met a lot of "Matts" in my day. Seems they're all over the place.

Matts are people who get caught up in their comfort zones, people who let their everyday habits run them, instead of them running their habits. Matts are people who just go through the motions...people who put in their time...people who "lead lives of quiet desperation," as Thoreau put it.

Hey, we all have comfort zones. No harm in that. But when we become slaves to our comfort zones, that's a different story. That's voluntary suffocation.

Remember Mary Lou Retton? She won a gold medal in gymnastics at the 1984 Olympics. Today she's one of the most sought-after motivational speakers in the country. Her topic? Breaking out of Comfort Zones:

*We all live our lives in comfort zones, avoiding risky situations, avoiding the potential to fail. It's real safe for us. But in order to get ahead, you've got to get out of your comfort zone. Try something new and see if it works. It may, it may not, but you'll never know if you don't try.*

One thing is for sure. As long as you're in your comfort zone, you're not growing. Sure, it's uncomfortable to venture outside your comfort zone. But believe me, it's the only way you'll grow!

Years ago I watched a made-for-TV movie called *Boy in a Bubble*, starring a young John Travolta. The movie was based on a true story about a kid who had to live in a totally sterilized environment because his immune system stopped working.

Doctors built a 10-foot-square, clear plastic sterilized bubble for the boy to live in. Everything that entered had to be germ free. People could see him and talk to him through the plastic bubble, but they could never enter his world for fear of passing along a fatal virus.

At the end of the movie the boy is faced with an agonizing choice. He can remain in the bubble and stay alive for years...alone, isolated from the rest of the world. Or he can choose to leave the bubble and live his life — no matter how brief — to the fullest.

What do you think the boy chose to do? Do you think he chose to live a longer life inside his sterilized comfort zone? .... Or did he choose to live a shorter — although happier — life on the outside?

What about you?...where would you choose to live?

More to the point, *where are you living?*

## Change: Friend Or Foe?

For the record, Travolta's character chose to leave the security of his bubble. He knew that in order to *truly live*, he had to leave his protective bubble and embrace life, no matter how short it was.

That movie reminds me of a conversation I had several years ago with Tommy Lasorda, manager of the Los Angeles Dodgers, during the filming of a television show I was producing. I asked Lasorda if he had any children, and he said yes, a daughter and a son. He went on to say his son had passed away a few months earlier. I said I was sorry and extended my condolences.

And then Lasorda said something to me that I've never forgotten: "Burke," he said. "My son was a little over 33 years old when he died. If God had come down from the heavens and appeared before me 33 years ago to tell me He was offering me a choice between having a son who would be taken from me before his 34th birthday...or not having a son so that I would be spared the pain of his death, I'd have chosen to have a son, no doubt about it. He's gone now, but my wife and I wouldn't give up those 33 years of joy we had while he was with us for anything in the world."

Lasorda's story is a perfect illustration of a universal truth: Pain is an unavoidable part of life, and the more you try to protect yourself from the pain of living, the more you smother the simple joys that life has to offer.

## From Cocoon To Butterfly

That's why it saddens me to see people retreat from the changes that technology brings instead of welcoming them.

Seems like more and more people are running from

reality, instead of facing it. Futurist Faith Popcorn even coined a term for this phenomenon: *Cocooning*.

Great word, cocoon. Nice and safe and warm in there. But given the choice between resisting change and staying in your cocoon...and embracing change and growing into a beautiful, soaring butterfly...what would you choose?

To quote Aldous Huxley, "Ignoring the facts doesn't make them any less true." And the fact is technology is changing the way we live, work and play, and those changes are happening faster today than ever before.

Just ask the executives at Smith Corona about the impact of technology. Smith Corona was a leading manufacturer of typewriters for over 100 years. Then personal computers exploded onto the scene, and during a 10-year period starting in 1983, typewriters were virtually replaced by 25 million PCs. In 1995 Smith Corona was forced to declare bankruptcy.

Technology is so powerful it can create billion-dollar industries almost overnight. Just look at cellular phones. In 1983, there were zero cellular phone subscribers. Ten years later, 16 million Americans were spending tens of billions of dollars a year on cellular phones.

Look, folks, change is everywhere. You can't hide from it by denying it or ignoring it. It's constant. Change doesn't necessarily cause good things or bad things to happen to people. How people *react* to change, however, can have good or bad consequences.

## Up In Smoke

A classic example of people suffering or prospering, depending on how they reacted to change, happened just across the bridge from me in Tampa, Florida.

At the turn of the century, Tampa was known as the cigar capital of the world. In fact, three generations of cigar workers lived and worked in a prosperous, bustling 20-square block section of town called Ybor City (pronounced EE-BORE CITY), named after Tampa's first cigar factory owner.

Ybor City was home to more than 60 cigar factories in the 1920s. Huge, 4-, 5- and 6-story brick factories housed thousands of immigrants who worked 10-hour days handrolling over 100 million cigars every year.

Cigar workers could make as much as $20 a week, a good wage back then, and the money supported hundreds of flourishing Ybor City businesses. Until the 1940s, the cigar was king and life was good in Ybor City.

After WWII, factory owners began replacing cigar workers with machines that would do the same work in a fraction of the time at a fraction of the cost. Best of all, machines never went on strike. Machines never called in sick or demanded a raise.

To make matters worse, cigar smoking fell out of favor, and the dreaded "C" word — *change* — stalked the streets of Ybor City. Men and women who knew nothing else but cigar making were out of jobs.

Houses went into foreclosure. Mothers took in

wash. Fathers drank. Families broke up. And Ybor City went from a boom town to a ghost town in 10 years.

## Proactive vs. Reactive

Lots of good people suffered as change swept over Ybor City. Change can be devastating to people who don't see it coming, or who don't admit to themselves that it's coming. The *reactive* citizens of Ybor City, the negative people who cursed the machines and longed for the good old days, suffered the most.

But what about the men and women who came back from the war and saw the handwriting on the factory wall? Were they really worse off because they were out of low-paying, dead-end jobs? Or better off because now they were *forced to break out of their comfort zones* and seek new opportunities in emerging industries.

The *proactive* citizens of Ybor City saw the end of the 10-hour days in hot, smelly factories as a blessing, not a curse.

Some went off to college on the GI Bill...and upon graduation entered the workforce during the most prosperous 25 years in our nation's history.

Some jumped on the technology bandwagon and took good-paying jobs with fast-growing telephone companies, utility companies and manufacturers.

Some learned a trade and found steady work as carpenters and plumbers.

And some scraped together enough money to open

a restaurant...a corner drug store...a flower shop...a clothing store...a neighborhood bank. For them, change wasn't a four-letter word. Change was a breath of fresh air, a chance to wash the stale smell of tobacco from their clothes, once and for all!

Take an honest look at your own life and ask this question: How would you like to wash your past clean and embark on a new life?

## Learn To Love Change

Tom Peters, management consultant to many Fortune 500 companies and author of *In Search of Excellence*, one of the best-selling business books in history, says this about change:

*Change is disruptive.... But it doesn't make any difference. You gotta do it anyway. We're in an era where, literally, to learn to love change is the only survival course.*

Ever hear the old saying, "Change is the only constant"? Today, that's true more than ever! It's like the story Steven Covey likes to tell at the beginning of his talk on the *Seven Habits of Highly Effective People*.

A night watchman on a huge battleship alerted the captain that their ship was headed directly toward a light in the distance. The captain immediately sent the message, "Change your course 10 degrees south."

A few minutes later came the reply, "Change your course 10 degrees north."

Perturbed, the captain signaled back, "I am a captain. Change your course south."

Five minutes later came the reply, "I am a seaman

first class. Change your course north."

Fuming, the captain sent one final message: "I demand you change your course. I'M ON A BATTLE-SHIP!"

"I strongly recommend you change your course," came the response. "I'm a lighthouse."

The moral of the story is pretty clear, isn't it? Technology is the lighthouse, and it's rather audacious of us to demand that technology slow down and move over so we can keep cruising straight ahead in our comfort zone.

If you were the captain of the battleship, what would you do? Hold your course...or change your course?

Well, each of us is the captain of our lives. We have a choice of changing our course and surviving...even flourishing, for that matter. Or staying our course and plunging headfirst into disaster.

As H. Jackson Brown, Jr. says in the best-selling *Life's Little Instruction Book*, "Never underestimate your power to change yourself. Never overestimate your power to change the world."

# 4

## Choice, Not Chance, Determines Your Destiny

*Opportunities can drop in your lap...*
*if you place your lap where opportunities drop.*
— Anonymous

Abraham Lincoln endured more than his share of misery during his lifetime. He grew up dirt poor and started working ten-hour days by age seven. Life didn't get any easier when he became an adult.

At age 22, he failed in business.

Age 24, he failed again in business.

Age 26, his beloved fiancee, Ann Rutledge, died.

Age 27, he suffered a nervous breakdown.

Ages 29, 31, 34, 39, 46, 47, and 49 he lost various elections.

While serving as president, he agonized over the Civil War...endured a bad marriage to an hysterical woman who nearly spent him into bankruptcy...and suffered endlessly when his favorite son, Willie, died before his 10th birthday.

Yet despite numerous personal and professional setbacks, Lincoln was generally a positive, upbeat man who loved to swap anecdotes and tell jokes at every opportunity.

When asked how he remained so cheerful in the face of constant adversity, Lincoln replied, "It's been my observation that people are just about as happy as they make up their minds to be."

## Same Event, Different Choices

Lincoln understood that it's not necessarily the circumstances that determine whether we are happy or sad, a success or a failure. Rather, it's how we *choose* to react to those circumstances.

If you've ever been caught in a traffic jam, you'll understand what I mean. Some drivers go ballistic, honking their horns...screaming...slamming car doors. While others turn a negative into a positive. They push back their seats, pop a cassette in the stereo (or crack open a book) and use the time to learn and grow, instead of whine and moan. Same event, different choices.

A while back I was stranded in an airport after a connecting flight was cancelled. The guy next to me paced the floor for hours, fuming and cursing everyone associated with the airline. By the time we boarded the next flight out, his face was beet red. His blood pressure must have been off the chart.

Know what I did? I used the time to jot down some ideas I'd been turning over in my mind. Those notes became the working outline for this book! Same event, different choices.

## Making Plans

Now, I'm not so naive as to think that we have a say in every single thing that happens to us. For sure, God gave us free will to choose our own way. But He also has His own divine plan, and my humble choices may or may not be in line with that plan.

Any time I get too full of myself, I remind myself of the joke I heard during a sermon years ago.

*Do you know how to make God laugh?*

*Tell Him your plans.*

The point is that there are some things we can choose...and there are some things that have been chosen for us. We don't, for example, have a choice over the weather. The nation was reminded of this truism in 1992 when Hurricane Andrew tore a path of destruction through much of Florida.

We can't choose how many hours are in the day...when the sun will rise and set...when we are ordained to die. We have no choice in these and a million other matters, so we might as well quit worrying about it.

On the other hand, we do have a choice in how we respond to each of these events, isn't that so? For example, I knew a married couple who chose to stay in their beachfront home and "ride out the storm" when Hurricane Andrew hit. Bad choice.

Amazingly, they survived the wrath of Andrew — although they emerged from their home very scared and very respectful of Mother Nature's awesome power! I guarantee you they'll be the first people to evacuate during the next hurricane alert!

When I say "Choice, not chance, determines your destiny," I'm referring to the hundreds of choices we make every day...and how those choices affect our lives.

## Living And Choosing

No doubt about it, the right to make your own choices is one of the greatest benefits of living in a free, prosperous society. True, most of the hundreds of choices we make every single day seem pretty insignificant at the time, like choosing between eating toast or cereal for breakfast.

But did you ever stop to think that each choice we make, no matter how big or how small, has a consequence? Over time, those little choices can add up to big consequences.

Smoking is a perfect example. If you choose to smoke one cigarette during your lifetime, the consequence is very small. If you choose, however, to smoke a pack of cigarettes a day for 30 years, the consequence could be lung cancer or a fatal heart attack.

If you think about it, who you are is determined by the choices you make. "Tell me who you hang out with and I'll tell you who you are," my mom always used to tell me. And she was right on!

When it's all said and done, you choose whether you weigh a lot or weigh a little...whether you've got a great attitude or a lousy one...whether your friends are the kind who pick you up or pull you down...whether you believe in Christ or believe in Buddha...whether you work for someone else or work for yourself.

Each time you make a choice, it's like making a deposit in the bank. Eventually, over time, all those deposits add up to who you are...how you look...how you feel...what you do...where you live...and last but not least, *what you own and what you earn!*

## Choosing Success

Louis L'Amour, the prolific author who wrote scores of novels about the Old West, summed up how each of us shapes our own destiny by the choices we make:

"Up to a point a man's life is shaped by environment, heredity, and movements and changes in the world about him. Then there comes a time when it lies within his grasp to shape the clay of his life into the sort of thing he wishes to be. Only the weak blame parents, their race, their times, lack of good fortune, or the quirks of fate. Everyone has it in his power to say, *This I am today; that I will be tomorrow."*

L'Amour's forthright wisdom boils down to this. Choices have consequences. Make good ones, you prosper. Make lousy ones, you suffer.

The Bible says the same thing in these five simple yet elegant words: *You reap what you sow.*

Folks, please, *please respect your power to choose!* Honor it…nurture it…and exercise it with love and wisdom. You can choose to be a good spouse and parent…you can choose to be thinner and healthier…you can choose to be positive and open-minded.

Above all, you can choose to be free. Free from a boss. Free to set your own hours. Free to earn what you're truly worth, instead of what your job description says you are worth.

## Meaningful Information, Purposeful Action

Think for a moment about the choice you made to open this book and read it. You could be watching TV instead…or flipping through *People* magazine to catch up on the latest celebrity gossip.

By choosing to read this book, however, you've proved you're after *meaningful information* rather than glossy entertainment — and make no mistake about it, in an information-driven world, meaningful information is king!

Did you know there's more information in a single issue of the *New York Times* than the average person was likely to come across in a lifetime during 17th-century England! Even more to the point, it's not what you know that counts — *it's what you do with what you know!* That's what I call *purposeful action.*

A perfect illustration of the power of putting information into action happened nearly 500 years ago to Christopher Columbus during one of his voyages to the New World.

In 1504 Columbus ordered his crew to anchor

their ship off the coast of Jamaica. The long voyage had depleted most of the on-board supplies, and Columbus' men were desperate for fresh food and water.

The native Jamaicans, however, refused to trade. Columbus begged and threatened, to no avail. He could have chosen to attack the natives, but he knew a battle was suicidal, for the island was heavily populated and the Jamaicans were well armed. The situation looked hopeless!

One night while reviewing his navigator's almanac, Columbus came across some potentially *meaningful information*. He discovered that a lunar eclipse was scheduled to occur within a few days.

Columbus mulled the information about the eclipse over in his mind, trying to devise a plan that would take advantage of knowledge that was unavailable to the less sophisticated Jamaicans. Columbus finally settled on a clever plan of *purposeful action* that literally saved the lives of the explorer and his crew.

Columbus arranged a meeting with the Jamaican leaders on the day of the eclipse, and warned them that if they continued to refuse to trade with him, he would have no choice but to use his magical powers to blot out the moon that night. And if they refused to trade with him the following day, he would call on the sun to drop fire on their villages.

The Jamiacans laughed at him and ignored the threat. That night, as the eclipse began, the Jamaicans stared in astonishment as the moon began slowly to disappear. The panic-stricken natives rushed to Columbus, who offered to restore the moon that night under one condition — they must bring fresh supplies to his ship immediately.

The Jamaicans accepted Columbus' offer without hesitation, and gasped in amazement as the moon reappeared...just as Columbus had promised.

## Choosing Wisely And Well

What do you think would have happened to Columbus if he didn't have the information about the eclipse...or if he had the information and didn't do anything with it? No doubt, it would have changed the course of history.

Information by itself is like a light switch in the "off" position. But look what happens when you add action to that information. By flicking the light switch to "on," its power is unleashed, and ...*voilá,* you have light!

One thing's for sure.

Whether you choose to switch on a light...finish this book...or become independent in a job-dependent world, the choice is yours — and yours alone.

May the rest of the information in this book help you choose wisely...and well.

# PART 2

---

# An American Addiction —
# Being Broke

# 5

## Being Broke Ain't No Joke!

*When the well is dry, we know the worth of water.*
— Benjamin Franklin

I can tell you from firsthand experience that being broke ain't no joke.

I know, 'cause I've been there, friend.

Forrest Gump says, "Being dumb ain't no box of chocolates." I'm here to tell ya that being broke ain't no box of chocolates, either. Know what it is?

*A box of unpaid bills!*

Put yourself in my shoes...How would you like to be out of work...$200,000 in debt...trying to support a two-year-old son and a pregnant wife? Talk about some sleepless nights!

In 1985 we rented a one-bedroom apartment furnished from garage sales. The family car was a beat-up, rusted-out Datsun I patched together with fiberglass.

Money was tight...so tight, in fact, that I couldn't afford $150 a month to pay our health insurance premiums...even with a pregnant wife.

## From Bad To Worse!

You guessed it! My wife Debbie started having contractions weeks before her due date. Twenty minutes apart...then 10...this was for real! We rushed to the hospital in time for Debbie to deliver our second son, Nathen, nine weeks before her due date.

He weighed only three pounds and required round-the-clock care for a month before we could bring him home.

We thank God every day that our son came through that ordeal without any side effects or long-term problems. I'm delighted to report that he's as healthy as a horse today and is very gifted and the most physical of our four children.

But Debbie and I still cringe when we think of the weeks following Nathen's release from the hospital. Not because we feared for his physical well being. Nathen was fine. Truth was, Nathen was the least of our problems.

## A Shoe Box Full Of Bills

It was our *fiscal well being* that had us both scared. The medical bills for Nathen kept coming in...and coming in. I put them all in a shoe box...and the bills spilled over into a second shoe box before the damage was done. To the tune of *over* $50,000!

Yep, now we owed over $250,000 at a time I couldn't even find the extra money to pay a monthly health insurance premium of $150! Here I was, closing down a failed conventional business, a cellular phone store…beating away the creditors…and I'm supposed to come up with $50,000? Unbelievable! I'm proud to say we eventually made good on those bills after I succeeded in an unconventional business of my own. But more about that later.

## Broke Is…

Remember all those "Happiness is…" definitions that were going around a few years ago? "Happiness is a sleeping puppy"…and "Happiness is a warm fire on a cold night."

Well, I've got some *broke is…* definitions for you.

*Broke is* being able to pay only the minimum on your monthly credit card balance.

*Broke is* renting instead of owning because you can't afford the down payment.

*Broke is* putting off going to that great new movie because it's cheaper to rent a video.

*Broke is* putting off that much-needed vacation until next year…again!

*Broke is* lying awake at night wondering how you're going to pay the rent.

Here's the perfect definition of being broke:

*Being broke is choosing between going deeper in debt or going without.*

## A Crash Course In Easy Credit

No doubt about it, the origin of the "being broke epidemic" sweeping this country is a highly contagious "virus" called *easy credit*. Let's look at America before this virus hit our country — and what happened once it started to spread.

It used to be that if you wanted to buy something, you worked real hard and saved your nickels and dimes until you had enough money to buy it. Up until the 1950s, that's the way most Americans bought stuff.

Psychologists called it "delayed gratification." You had to exercise discipline for months, even years, in order to buy what you wanted. Most people learned to go without. And pretty much everyone lived within their means.

Oh, sure, if you had a good job, you could get a loan to buy a home. Or a new car. Maybe even buy a refrigerator or washer and dryer at Sears on credit. But that was about it.

In 1952 America was introduced to a new way of buying. Instead of "save now, buy later," this new way encouraged consumers to "buy now, pay later." All you had to do was plunk down a little piece of plastic called a credit card, and *violá*...you could own now and then work real hard later to pay it off.

Needless to say, Americans took to credit cards like a fish to water. Instant gratification...Ain't it great? The whole country jumped on the credit card bandwagon. Before we knew it, every working adult had a credit card...or two...or five! We used credit cards to pay for gas...furniture...airline tickets...you name it. (I know 'cause I've been there! When I was broke, I managed to run up a $1,000 grocery bill at the local Chevron gas station!)

The whole country fell victim to Oscar Wilde's witticism, "The only way to get rid of a temptation is to yield to it." It wasn't long before Americans were living beyond their means.

According to *USA Today*, 40 percent—that's four out of every 10 Americans — *spend more than they make!* How do they do that? Can you say, "CHARGE IT!"? No wonder people are broke!

Today, credit card debt has become a national epidemic. We're a nation of 265 million people...with 800 million credit cards in circulation. In 1994 alone, Americans charged almost $500 billion on credit cards!

Now, that's fine and dandy if you pay off your monthly credit card bills. But the reality is, most of us don't. We pay the first line...the minimum. Only problem is, at 15 percent or even 20 percent interest rate, the only ones making any headway are the credit card companies — and they're making out like bandits.

Remember my definition of being broke?

*Being broke is choosing between going deeper in debt or going without.*

With 40 percent of the population living beyond their means, it's pretty obvious Americans are choosing to go deeper into debt than to live without, right? It's a sad commentary on America, the richest country in the world, that millions of us are spending ourselves into being broke!

Don't get me wrong. I'm not saying everyone should pay cash for everything. I have a mortgage and several credit cards, too. What I'm saying is that easy credit is a velvet pillow that can make you more comfortable...or can suffocate you, depending on how you use it — or abuse it.

If you're like most Americans, you're sinking your head deeper and deeper into that velvet pillow. A recent poll by Merrill Lynch revealed that the average 50-year-old has only $2,300 in savings.

The experts say you'll need at least a million dollars in savings to earn $50,000 a year in retirement. Yet most Americans can't write a check from savings for $3,000? That's a shame! And there's NO excuse for it!

## How Being Broke Affects Us

I'm not saying that money is the key to happiness. But like a friend of mine says, "The more money you have, the easier it is to get the key made."

Have you ever stopped to think how being broke affects people? It's worse than bad. It's devastating!

Being broke means more stress...more arguments with your spouse...more physical illness...more bouts of depression...more anger...more worries... more fears...yeah, lots more fears!

Ever hear the story about Big Jake? I always think of that story when I hear about someone with money problems.

A traveling salesman stops off at a small-town tavern to quench his thirst after a hard day on the road. Suddenly, a terrified man runs in shouting, "Run for your lives! Big Jake's comin'!"

As everybody scatters, an enormous man kicks down the front door, throws the chairs and tables to the side, grabs the salesman by the shirt collar and screams, "Get me a drink, NOW!"

The terrified salesman runs behind the bar and quickly hands the giant a quart of whiskey. The huge man empties the contents in one gulp and then proceeds to eat the bottle.

Nearly paralyzed with fear, the salesman stammers, "Can I get you another one?"

"Nope, I gotta run," grunts the giant. "Didn't you hear? Big Jake's comin'!"

Well, when you're broke, seems like just when you thought you had big worries...that things couldn't get any worse...you learn that Big Jake hasn't even arrived yet!

Hey, we're all gonna have some rain in our lives. That's part of life, like it or not. But when you've got money, it's a lot easier to stay dry 'cause you can afford to patch the roof or buy a new umbrella. It's like the comedian Joe E. Lewis used to say, "There's only one thing money won't buy, and that's poverty."

## Fortunately, Broke Is Temporary

Look, there's no shame in being broke. The only shame is staying broke and *accepting* it as a way of life. Especially if you live in America!

If you really and truly want to break the cycle of being broke, you can...because broke is a temporary situation. It's not a death sentence unless you act as your own judge and jury and condemn yourself.

Hey, you know why people from all over the world are sneaking across our borders...riding makeshift rafts across shark-infested waters to America? Because they'd rather be broke and free than poor and enslaved, that's why!

They don't call it the land of opportunity for nothing, you know.

Tired of being broke? Feeling pretty sorry for yourself? Well, I'm here to tell you there's a big, BIG difference between being broke and being poor. To fully appreciate the difference, all you have to do is answer this question: How would you feel if there were no hope of ever escaping from being broke? Depression and misery would be your two constant companions, wouldn't they?

When being broke is all you've ever known...all you'll ever know...and all there is...it becomes a permanent condition called poverty.

Poverty is constant.

Poverty is suffocating.

Poverty is permanent.

You see, I thoroughly understand what poverty does to people because I grew up surrounded by poverty. Before I moved to the U.S. at the age of 14, I spent my early years in Jamaica and Ecuador, where poverty was the rule, not the exception.

For years I saw poverty every single day...real, unrelenting, merciless poverty. And I wouldn't wish it on my worst enemy!

The point is, before you start crying about the lack of real opportunity in this country today, let's look at what millions of other people outside North America are facing.

Remember the old adage, "I felt sorry for myself because I didn't have any shoes. Then I met a man who didn't have any feet."

Before you start feeling sorry for yourself because you're too broke to buy new shoes ... let's take a look at how true poverty cuts people off at the ankles.

# 6

## Being Broke vs. Being Poor

*I bargained with life for a penny,*
*Only to learn dismayed.*
*That any wage I would have asked of life,*
*Life would have paid.*

— Anonymous

*"If you want to know about water, don't ask a fish."*

That's what the brilliant social critic Marshall McLuhan used to say when his views were challenged by an industry "expert." Experience had taught McLuhan that when people get too close to something, they can't really step back and take an honest look at it.

The same could be said about the U.S., "the land of opportunity" to millions of foreigners.

*"If you want to know about opportunity, don't ask an American."*

The newspapers and TV news shows are full of doom and gloom reports about layoffs and the shrinking job market. Truth is, opportunity surrounds us like water surrounds a fish. We're only six percent of the world's population, but we're the world's richest country and, by far, the world's biggest consumer.

53

If you can't find a product or service to sell to Americans, you aren't looking very hard. Fact is, the Japanese, the Chinese, the Germans and everyone else are jumping all over themselves trying to figure out what Americans will buy next.

Compared to most people in this world, we've got it made.

## It's All Relative

Did you know that only 5 percent of the U.S. economy today feeds and houses every American citizen? That means that the rest of our economy — 95 percent — is made up of *non-essential goods and services,* most of which didn't exist 10 years ago.

Just imagine. Only 5 percent of the economy goes to cover our basic *needs* — food and shelter. The rest goes to buy all the stuff that gives us pleasure. Or status. I mean, do we really need a new car to survive? Or a TV set? How about two TV sets, which most U.S. homes have? And on and on.

What makes North America so wealthy is we spread the money around by spending it on things we *want* but don't really need, like $20 haircuts, $50 dinners and $100 tennis shoes.

Now I'm not saying we don't have poor people in America. We do. But it's *relative poverty* as opposed to absolute poverty. Look, the simple fact is this: Any North American who is not seriously mentally impaired would be hard pressed to starve to death. Can't say that in Somalia, can you?

Are there homeless folks living in cardboard boxes

on the streets of our cities? Yes.

Are there kids who go to bed hungry every night? Sadly, yes.

Are there two, sometimes three families living in abandoned buildings without running water and electricity? Yes, again.

Hey, situations like this are sad. Even tragic. But very few would tell you their situation is hopeless.

Broke, yes.

In relative poverty, yes.

In absolute poverty, no.

Let's get real. Ever heard about anyone in this country floating on a makeshift raft to Haiti with the hope of finding a better life? How many Americans swim across the Rio Grande at night to find work as domestics in Mexico?

Let me tell you what *absolute poverty* is. The average yearly income in Haiti is $250. THAT'S $250 DOLLARS A YEAR!!! Will it jump to $600 next year and $1,000 the next? Not a chance! That's absolute poverty, plain and simple.

## Seeing Is Believing

Like I said earlier, I grew up in places where absolute poverty was the rule, not the exception. In Ecuador at least half of the population lives in absolute poverty — literally millions of people go to bed hungry most nights.

My family was fortunate. Although my father lost millions of dollars overnight when Castro's communist government took over Cuba, my father still managed to provide us with an above-average lifestyle.

But I grew up surrounded by poverty. I remember playing with the children of a farmhand in Ecuador. They lived in a house built from cast off wooden crates. They had no electricity...no running water ...no indoor plumbing...no stove...and flies everywhere.

They lived in a neighborhood surrounded by "houses" just like theirs. Fact is, 80 percent of the houses in the city, maybe more, were shanties. You see, in South America, poverty isn't something to be ashamed of...or even denied, for that matter. Poverty just is. Unrelenting, unending, absolute poverty.

Oh, sure, a few lucky ones escape from poverty. Very few. One out of a million athletic boys will become a soccer star. One out of a million pretty girls will marry a rich husband. But the majority are born into poverty, live in poverty and die in poverty.

## Compared To Other Countries, Our "Poor" Have It Made

According to the U.S. Census Bureau, there are nearly 40 million poor Americans. Wow! That's a lot of poor people. So why do I keep hearing the U.S. has one of the highest standards of living in the world?

It's not because we have so many poor people...it's because the Census Bureau defines the word "poor" in such a way that it includes a whole bunch of people who are doing great compared to the rest of the world!

Check out these facts about so-called "poor Americans":

- The Bureau defines a "poor American" as a family of four with an income of just over $14,000 or less a year. (Compare that to $600 per year for most of China!)
- Nearly 40 percent of all "poor American" households own their own homes.
- The average "poor American" lives in twice as much living space as the average Japanese and four times the space as the average Russian.
- Almost three out of four "poor Americans" own their own cars.
- Over 90% of "poor Americans" own at least one color TV.
- Far from being malnourished, the average "poor American" is more likely to be overweight than middle class people.

That's some kind of poor, huh? Let's face it, compared to the rest of the world, poor Americans have it made. And the best news of all is this: Poor Americans don't have to stay that way.

## Being Broke vs. Being Poor

Remember: Unlike poverty, which is permanent, being broke is temporary. I'll never forget when my wife Debbie and I were up to our eyeballs in debt and down to our last dollar...renting a tiny one-bedroom apartment...driving a rusted-out old bomb...without health insurance...$250,000 in debt...and I was 50 pounds overweight, to boot! We were broke and down…but not poor and out!

You see, I believed with all my heart that some-day…some way…somehow, we'd have money. And a home. And a bright future for us and the kids.

Even if you lived during the Great Depression, the absolute worst economic period in the history of our country, you'd be better off than most people living today in Ecuador. Or Haiti. Or Rwanda. Or Somalia. Or even Russia. Absolute poverty is the rule rather than the exception in these countries — and in scores of other countries all over the globe.

Would you say there's a little or a lot of opportunity for average poor citizens to better themselves in Third World countries? Little to none, right? On the other hand, America is loaded with opportunity! Opportunity is all around us. But it comes with a price, folks. No one hands it to us. We have to pursue it.

Hey, the Declaration of Independence doesn't give you the *right to happiness.* It only gives you the right to *pursue happiness.* Likewise, free enterprise doesn't give you the *right to wealth* but *the right* to *pursue wealth!*

## Right In Your Own Backyard

It's like the story Rich Devos, co-founder of Amway, tells in his best-selling book, *Believe.* A man calls up a realtor and asks him to sell his house. The realtor comes by, takes some measurements and notes, and tells the owner to look for the advertisement in the

Sunday paper.

Sure enough, come Sunday the homeowner scans the real estate section and reads this ad:

> *Gorgeous 4-bedroom, 3-bath dream home on one-acre landscaped lot. Walking distance to good schools and great shopping. Lovely screened-in pool. Lots of extras. Must see it to believe it! Call for appointment.*

Immediately, the homeowner called the realtor and shouted, "I just read your ad for my house, and I want you to take it off the market immediately!"

"Did I say something wrong in the ad?" the stunned realtor asked.

"No," replied the homeowner, "not at all. When I read your ad, I suddenly realized I already owned the home I'd always dreamed of."

Like the homeowner, sometimes we need to be reminded that it doesn't get any better than what we have right here in our own backyard.

## Drowning In A Flood of Opportunity

When I hear politicians and union bosses talk about the need for more jobs, I just want to scream. Trying to prop up ailing industries with price supports so more jobs won't be lost is like trying to paste dead leaves on trees so that summer won't end. You're only kidding yourself!

The answer to reducing layoffs is not to find a more secure job. Let's face it, secure jobs don't exist anymore (if, in fact, they ever did). The answer to reducing lay-offs is to increase the number of people who work for themselves...self-employment instead of employment.

Does that mean that everyone who has a job should resign tomorrow and go into business for himself? Of course not, because there will always be people willing to settle for a job. Some people just don't have the confidence...or ambition...or desire...to make a go of it on their own.

Truth is, I think jobs serve a very valuable function in a free enterprise system. I don't know of one successful business owner or entrepreneur who hasn't worked for someone else at one time or another (just as I don't know any who would go back to working for someone else).

To me, a job is not an end in itself. At best, a job is a necessary stepping stone from answering to a boss to being your own boss. For ambitious, enterprising workers, a job can act as a paid internship. In a job, you earn while you learn. That's like getting paid for going to school. Can't beat it!

A job's only as good as the person performing it, isn't that true? Therefore, it stands to reason that if you're real good at performing your job, then you're the issue, not the job...you have value in the marketplace, not the job.

That's why I tell people with jobs to keep their noses to the grindstone and their eye out for opportunity. In the words of a successful entrepreneur, *"There is no future in any job. The future lies in the person who holds the job."*

# 7

## Are You A Victim...Or A Victor?

*When an archer misses the mark, he turns and looks for the fault within himself. Failure to hit the bulls-eye is never the fault of the target. To improve your aim — improve yourself.*

— Gilbert Arland

On my way to work every morning I pass a billboard that pretty well sums up the American character of late, I'm sad to say.

The billboard shows an illustration of five crying babies sitting side by side. Each baby is pointing a finger at the baby to his or her right. The caption reads:

THAT'S RIGHT AMERICA...
IT'S ALWAYS SOMEONE ELSE'S FAULT!

I have no idea who paid for the billboard. But when I find out, I'm going to make a donation so they'll keep it up a little longer. Hey, let's face it, we're becoming a nation of crybabies...a country populated by what I call "voluntary victims."

61

## The Victim Game

The voluntary victim game is a nasty little game that's replaced baseball as the national pastime. The game has a million variations, but all of them boil down to one basic formula:

POOR ME. BECAUSE I'M A VICTIM,
THE WORLD OWES ME A LIVING.

This line of reasoning reminds me of a Peanuts cartoon where Snoopy is sitting in the pouring rain, feeling sorry for himself. He says, "There's nothing more pathetic than a little dog sitting in the rain."

Lucy walks by carrying an umbrella, glances over at Snoopy and says, "There's nothing more pathetic than a dog too stupid to get in out of the rain."

In the final panel Snoopy...still sitting in the rain, sad and all alone...says, "Either way, I'm pathetic..."

Marion Rudin Frank, a clinical psychologist in Philadelphia, says this about chronic complainers: "By repeatedly bemoaning their fate, chronic complainers cast themselves as victims...which is nothing more than self-sabotage."

If that's not bad enough, complainers attract other complainers. You've heard the old expression, "Misery loves company," haven't you? That's why there's so many national chapters of the Ain't-It-Awful Club — and why I refuse to associate with negative people.

Truth is, voluntary victims don't *really* want to fix problems because they don't *really* care about solutions. The role of the victim absolves them of any responsibility for fixing a problem...and secretly they enjoy the attention they get from whining.

Now it's fine to express our complaints and feel down now and then. We all do from time to time. It helps us get it out of our system. But let's face the facts — *playing the victim never solves anything.* All it does is add fuel to the misery bonfire. At some point you gotta get up, wipe your nose and get on with it.

## Life Isn't Fair

Now I know some of your are thinking to yourselves, *"Yeah, but walk a mile in my shoes! Life isn't fair, Burke. My parents got divorced when I was young...we were always broke when I was a kid...I grew up on the wrong side of the tracks...I've always had a weight problem..."* and so on and so forth.

Where does it say in the U.S. Constitution that you have a God-given right to feel sorry for yourself? It's not a right — it's a *justification* for not taking responsibility for your actions!

Hey, no one said life was fair. There are some people who were dealt terrible hands, no doubt about it. Let's say you've had a whole bunch of bad breaks. I'm sure you've had some pretty good breaks, too, like living in the United States of America during the late 20th century, for starters. Billions of people all over the world would trade places with you in a heartbeat. So don't take living in this great country of ours for granted!

If you think you've had some bad breaks, then listen to the story of a guy named W. Mitchell. Then maybe things won't seem so bad, after all.

One cold, wet night, W. Mitchell took a horrible

spill on his motorcycle, rupturing the gas tank. The leaking gas ignited and Mitchell received third-degree burns over 65 percent of his body. In the hospital he was in constant pain. He couldn't pick up a spoon, dial a phone or go to the bathroom without help.

It took 16 surgeries and hundreds of hours of painful therapy for Mitchell to recover enough to go back to work. To his credit, after all that pain and suffering, Mitchell was back piloting his own airplane only four months later!

Despite a scarred face and limited use of his hands, he teamed up with a couple friends and co-founded a wood-burning stove company that became one of the largest private employers in Vermont. Talk about courage.

Great story of triumph, right? Hold on, 'cause it gets worse. Four years after his motorcycle accident, Mitchell's plane crashed, crushing his backbone. He was paralyzed for life from the waist down. Talk about unfair! After all that pain...all that suffering...all those setbacks...all those limitations, did Mitchell say, "Hey, what's the use. Someone up there must have it in for me. I'll just give up!"?

No way. He campaigned for mayor from his wheelchair...and won! He even ran for U.S. Congress. Know what his slogan was? "Not just another pretty face." Talk about turning a negative into a positive!

He took up white water rafting...fell in love and married...and earned a master's degree. When he was interviewed on *The Today Show*, he said, "Before I was paralyzed there were 10,000 things I could do. Now there are 9,000 things. I can either dwell on the 1,000 things I lost...or focus on the 9,000 I have left."

The next time you start to fall into that voluntary victim role, think of W. Mitchell. If that doesn't break up your private "pity party," you deserve to drown in your sorrows.

## No Excuses

Years ago a very successful businessman said something to me that I've thought about hundreds of times since. He said, *"You can make money or you can make excuses. But you can't make both at the same time."*

Then he proceeded to tell the story about a 63-year- old man named Harlan who had every excuse in the world to play the role of a victim — but chose to become a victor instead! At one time Harlan owned a restaurant-motel-service station business he'd built up over the years. He was offered nearly $200,000 cash for the business, but turned down the offer because he wasn't quite ready to retire yet.

Two years later the state built a new superhighway bypassing his business. Within a year Harlan lost everything. Here he was, 65 years old, flat broke, and no income other than a small monthly Social Security check to live on.

He could have sued the state for destroying his business. But he didn't.

He could have taken to the bottle, drowning himself in his sorrows 'cause he was too old to start over. But he didn't.

Instead of playing victim, Harlan took stock in himself. The only thing he knew how to do well was cook chicken. Maybe he could sell that knowledge to someone else.

So he kissed his wife goodbye, loaded up his battered old car with a pressure cooker and his special recipe, and set out to sell his idea to the world. It was tough going, and he often slept in his car because there wasn't enough money for a hotel room.

Restaurant after restaurant turned him down...Harlan suffered 100, 200. 300 rejections before he found someone to believe in his dream. A few years later he opened the first of what would become thousands of successful restaurants located around the world.

The man was Harlan Sanders. Most likely you know him better by his more recognizable name — Colonel Sanders, the legend behind Kentucky Fried Chicken.

Because Colonel Sanders didn't use his age or his business failure as an excuse to give up, today his name is recognized around the world.

Because he remained true to his life-long conviction that starting and running your own business was the only way to go, he emerged a victor, not a victim!

## The Fourth Wave: Age Of The Entrepreneur

Now, I can hear the voluntary victims clearing their throats and mumbling, *"Hey, we all can't build fast-food empires like Colonel Sanders."*

True...but nothing's stopping you from taking your foot off first and making a run at owning your own business, is there? And don't give me that old song and dance that you've never really thought about owning your own business, either. Because I know that somewhere deep inside just about every one of us lies the dream to run our own show and call our own shots, isn't that true?

Check this out: *USA Today* recently reported the findings of a questionnaire asking if Americans were interested in owning their own business. Know what percentage of people ages 25 - 44 were very interested in owning their own business?

*Ninety-six percent!* Wow!

Do you know what that tells me? It tells me that most people believe there's an *intelligent alternative to having a job!*

That's why I coined the term "The Fourth Wave: Age of the Entrepreneur" to describe what's happening right now, today! More and more people are choosing to go into business for themselves...and I predict the self-employment trend will not only continue to grow, but will explode in the coming decade.

Why? Certainly, lack of job security is one big reason. Massive layoffs sent a message to American workers that lifetime employment is no longer part of the deal.

Money's another big reason. According to one study, three out of four millionaires became wealthy by owning their own business.

## Human Nature

However, I believe that humans are born with two fundamental drives that can't be denied or ignored. One, humans have an inborn need to *build* or *create*. And two, humans have an inborn need to *own*.

If those two words don't get you juiced, then you might as well put this book down and go grab the

67

Sunday comics, because I won't be telling you anything you'd want to hear.

If you've seen a movie sometime during the past 20 years, you know the name Steven Spielberg. He's directed some of the biggest box office hits in history, including the *Indiana Jones* series, *Jaws*, *E.T.*, *Jurassic Park*, and *Schindler's List*, among others.

The guy's got to be worth hundreds of millions of dollars. For years he worked for a studio called MCA. Despite the fact that MCA loved him...and he loved them...he left to start his own studio.

At the time, Spielberg and MCA were both making an absolute fortune. So why would one of the wealthiest, most sought-after directors in the history of Hollywood decide to leave MCA and plunk down $30 million to start a company of his own?

Listen to what Spielberg says about what motivated him to start up his own movie studio with a couple of very talented, very rich friends in the movie business, Jeffrey Katzenberg and David Geffen:

> *"The idea of building something from the ground up, where I could actually be a co-owner, where I don't rent, I don't lease, I don't option but actually own — that appeals to me."*

Notice the key words...*Building...Own*. He didn't say he wanted to make more money. He didn't say he was afraid of getting fired. He said he wanted to create and own.

When it's all said and done, that's what we all want to do, isn't it?

# 8

## The Rise And Fall Of The Late, Great Job

*You don't feel like a man if you don't have a job.*
*You don't feel right if all you're doing is making*
*withdrawals and not making deposits.*
— Hal McRae, *fired baseball manager*

*Downsizing.*

You've just got to love business jargon, don't you? *Downsizing.*

Seems like no one is *fired* or *laid off* anymore. It's a kinder, gentler world, right?

The corporate hatchet men even improved on the word downsizing. Now they call it *rightsizing.* Follow their line of reasoning. Let's say you were a hard-working, productive employee for 13 years. Through some Wall Street hocus pocus, the company is bought out and sold off. The new owner cuts 20 percent of the employees.

So, you're tellin' me that since 20 percent of the employees have been *downsized*, the company is *rightsized*? Does that mean it was *wrongsized* for 13 years? Ever feel like you're living in a George Carlin routine?

I just came across my all-time favorite business-speak word for job losses. *De-jobbed.*

Right there in *Fortune* magazine in an article called, "The End of the Job." The article states, "Many organizations are today well along the path to being de-jobbed."

Next thing you know undertakers won't say someone died...or even passed away. They'll say your loved one has been "de-lifed." What's goin' on here?

Fact is, if you have a job on Monday, you can be *de-jobbed* on Tuesday 'cause you're *de-pendent* on someone else for your income. And that's *de-pressing.*

Used to be they'd fire the person and keep the position. Today, they fire both the worker and the job. Get this. Over half the jobs lost in the 90s are gone forever. Poof. Disappeared. De-jobbed, indeed.

## The Evolution Of The Job

To find out what's happening to jobs all over the world, we need to understand how this thing called a "job" came about in the first place. Futurist Alvin Toffler, author of the international best-seller *Future Shock,* observes that civilization has undergone three great eras of change — Toffler calls them waves — that define the way we live and work.

In the First Wave, the *Agricultural Age*, societies moved from being centered around primitive hunting and gathering to farming.

The Second Wave, the *Industrial Age*, began 300 years ago in the factories in England and had its heyday during and shortly after WWII.

The Third Wave, the *Information Age,* was firmly established in this country during the mid-1950s, when, for the first time, white-collar workers out-numbered blue-collar workers.

Now let's look at the kinds of jobs people did in each of these ages and what that means to us today.

## Giant Waves On A Sea Of Change

During the Agricultural Age, jobs were chores that everyone in the family was assigned to do. Milk the cows...plow the field...butcher the hogs. You get the idea. That's why farmers had big families...gave them lots of cheap labor. When this country was founded, 90 percent of the population lived and worked on farms. People didn't have jobs. They *did jobs.* The Agricultural Age in this country has nearly run its course, evidenced by the fact that today only two per-cent of Americans live and work on farms.

Then came the Industrial Revolution and a whole new way of organizing work. As factories opened, farmers' sons and daughters ran off to the city to find work and excitement. *How ya' gonna keep 'em down on the farm, after they've seen Par-ree?* the WWI song goes.

Factories paid workers more than they'd earn milk-ing the family cow for "free," but there was a price to pay. People were treated like machines. A typical Industrial Age job was to put this nut on that bolt, over and over and over again. Even a dumb farmer's son could do that, right? Don't think. Just do the job.

So through the 1800s and up to the present day,

more and more people started to *have jobs*. Having a job became a way of organizing work...indeed, of organizing entire cultures, as the industrialized countries began building their lives around the job. Just look at how the job influenced virtually everything we did.

We left school or the military and *got a job*.

We moved from our hometowns to new cities *in search of a better job*.

We nagged at our kids to do well in school so they could *get a good job*.

We joined unions to improve the pay and *working conditions in our job*.

As the job became more and more entrenched in our minds, we became more and more dependent on getting a job and keeping it. Phrases like job training...job history...job hunting...job application...job corps...entered our language. We even created a name for people who didn't have jobs — *jobless*.

In the 20th century our jobs became synonymous with who we were: *I'm a teacher...I'm an accountant...I'm a carpenter*. The evolution of the job was complete, as the meaning gradually changed over the last 2,000 years from what we did .. to what we had...to *who we were!*

## The Third Wave Comes Crashing In

Only one problem. The thing that created the job in the first place — technology — started gobbling up our jobs like a giant Pac Man. In the 1970s and '80s, robots took over the jobs of blue-collar workers. In the 1990s, personal computers took over the jobs of white-collar workers. And here's the American worker, left standing in the rain holding a pink slip and two weeks' severance pay wondering, "What happened?"

What happened was this: An unexpected Third Wave called the Information Age hit us full force while we were asleep, washing away most of the jobs left over by the fading Industrial Age.

That's why we've got out-of-work engineers driving taxi cabs. Accountants leading aerobics classes. Architects waiting on tables.

Like any natural disaster, the damage wouldn't have been nearly as devastating if we'd been warned ahead of time. But let's face it, most Americans today are still using the success model that worked so well in the Industrial Age because that's what we've been told would work.

The old success formula went like this: There are only so many good jobs waiting out there. In order to get one, you'll have to go to college and learn all about the job you want. When you graduate, you'll need to start at the bottom of the job ladder and then work your way up to the middle, maybe even the top of the job ladder.

You put in your time...pay your dues...keep your nose clean...and you'll get two paychecks a month, a home in the 'burbs and a nice pension at 65. You might have said, "OK, this trade-off sounds fair enough. It worked for dad after WWII, why not me?"

So the baby-boom generation went off to college...and entered the workforce...and started climbing the ladder. But the rungs of the ladder got further apart...and the ladder got longer and longer. And in the 1980s, the corporations couldn't keep up their end of the deal. That's when the layoffs began, and they ain't over yet.

Now, the children of the baby-boomers, a whole new generation of young people we call "Generation X-ers," are looking at what happened to their parents. Mom and Dad are lecturing about the go-to-school-and-get-a-good-job success formula while the kids are looking at them with their arms crossed.

> *"Hey, Dad,"* asks Junior. *"If that's the way to do it, why isn't it working for you? Why are you looking for your fourth job in the last five years if that's the way to do it, huh? IF IT DOESN'T WORK FOR YOU, WHAT MAKES YOU THINK IT'S GONNA WORK FOR ME?"*

## Are You Looking In The Right Place?

Did you ever stop to think that having a job isn't the answer? That instead of looking to work for someone else, we should be looking into working for ourselves!

It reminds me of the story of the monkey and the Coca-Cola tree. One day a bright, ambitious monkey was walking through a rain forest far from his home village when he decided to take a rest under a huge shade tree. As he sat down and leaned against the trunk, his hand brushed a half-filled Coca-Cola bottle left behind by an expedition.

The monkey picked up the bottle and drank it down. "That's the most delicious juice I've ever tasted," he said to himself. "And you don't even have to peel the fruit! I know all of the monkeys in the world will love this exotic new juice. I must climb this tree and pick more of these to take back to my village."

He scurried all over the huge tree, but could not find another bottle of Coke. "This tree must have been picked clean by the monkeys in this forest," he thought to himself. "But that won't stop me. I'll keep searching until I find the Coca-Cola tree."

So he wandered through the rain forest, searching desperately for the mysterious Coca-Cola tree. Days turned into weeks...weeks into months...and months into years...until the monkey finally returned home empty-handed.

He became the joke of the village, a bitter, disillusioned old primate rambling on and on about the exotic Coca-Cola juice that grew on rare trees in the rain forest.

The monkey had the right idea (like most of us). But he was looking in the wrong place! He failed because his assumption was dead wrong. He *assumed* the Coca-Cola bottle dropped from the tree. That assumption doomed him to failure. Had he discovered the *true origin* of Coca-Cola, he would have become one rich monkey!

I agree with the Biblical saw, "Search and you shall find." But you're not going to find diamonds searching in a sandbox! You have to search in the right places!

Aren't millions of Americans acting like the monkey when they search for independence in the job tree? Aren't we doomed to failure, or at best mediocrity, by assuming a *job* will be our ticket to the American Dream of freedom...financial security...and personal fulfillment ?

So, we educate ourselves for the *right job*...or we re-train for a *new job*...and we get fired and sit at home until we stumble into still *another job.* No wonder the average worker in this country has 10-12 different jobs in four to five different careers before retirement.

*Maybe, just maybe*, we should take a serious look at our assumptions.

*Maybe, just maybe*, we're better off working for ourselves than working for someone else.

*Maybe, just maybe*, it's time to become independent in a job-dependent world.

## Who's Gonna Do The Work?

*Come on, Burke. If everyone takes your advice and goes into business for themselves, who's gonna do the work? Somebody's got to take the jobs, right?*

Slow down. I'm not saying there won't be any jobs. There's all kinds of jobs out there. Just open the Sunday paper to the classifieds. Help wanted ads will spill out all over your lap... ads for low-paying, unskilled, boring, dead-end jobs. But where's the future in that?

There are even some jobs for highly skilled professionals, like doctors and engineers and the like. A good friend of mine says his law firm is hiring. Starting pay is $25,000 for the "privilege" of working 100-hour weeks...and praying that the senior partners like you enough to invite you to pay the firm $100,000 or more for the privilege of becoming a partner!

And to think our best and brightest are lining up to go to law school. Thanks, but no thanks. Our best and brightest should be preparing to take advantage of opportunities instead of going back to graduate school in hopes of getting a better job.

## Change Is The Only Constant

Thanks to increasing technology, the world is changing faster and faster than ever before. Love it or hate it, that's just the way it is.

Just take a look at how technology has changed farming, for example. A century ago farms were worked mostly by hand. At the turn of this century 60 out of every 100 jobs in this country were farm-related. Today only two out of every 100 Americans work on farms, *yet farms are 1,000 times more productive than they were a century ago.*

Are there still farm jobs? Of course...just not as many. And unless you own the farm, they sure don't pay very well. The fact of the matter is, what happened to farming 100 years ago is happening to American business today. Technology is improving productivity at the expense of jobs. First the blue-collar jobs in the '80s. Then the white-collar jobs in the '90s. What's in store for the year 2000 and beyond? The Golden Age of Entrepreneurship, that's what!

## The Got-To-Get-A-Job Mentality

I'm saying the job that we've been taught to seek...*the job that we've been conditioned to expect — lifetime employment, challenging, high pay, great benefits, cushy retirement package — no longer exists.* Oh, sure, the occasional company will take advantage of your talent, enticing you with the "golden handcuffs" of long-term promises, while in reality only delivering short-term paychecks.

Empty promises aside, the days of lifetime employment went out with penny loafers and poodle skirts. Remember: The average American will have 10 to 12 jobs in four to five career areas in his lifetime. What's the chance that you or someone you know will work for the same company for 45 years? One in a million, maybe.

Check this out. Know who the biggest private employer in the U.S. is today? General Motors? General Electric? AT&T? Nope.

The answer is Manpower Temporary Services. What do they do? Assign people to a job and then reassign them to another job when the first one's done. How do you like that for job security?

*So, Burke, are you saying that if I don't aspire to becoming a permanent "Rent-A-Cop" or a "Kelly Girl," I'm doomed to under-employment?*

No, not at all. That's the good news. That's the

great news! Just as jobs as we know them are disappearing, **opportunities are exploding like never before!**

Unfortunately, opportunities, unlike jobs, usually don't advertise themselves in newspapers.

Fortunately, opportunities, unlike jobs, can be fun and creative and very profitable!

Most fortunately, opportunities are ever-abundant in the free enterprise system!

## What Business Are You In?

Years ago the railroad industry was king. Vast fortunes were made in the 1800s as the railroads served a growing nation by moving people and products all over the country.

But the railroad barons made a fatal mistake. They thought they were in the railroad business. What they were really in was the transportation business, and they lost out to trucks and the airlines. Railroad owners, investors and employees missed golden opportunities because they were short-sighted.

The same can be said for the average American. We think we're in the *job business*. But what we're really in is the *opportunity business*. And the ultimate opportunity is found in the free enterprise system.

Statistics show that 60 percent of Americans are three months away from being flat, out-on-the-street broke. Now, what got them to this point in their lives? The job road, right?

Doesn't common sense tell you that if the job road is NOT heading in the direction you want to go, you need to take a different road?  Like I always say, "If you continue to do the things you've always done, you'll continue to get the things you've always gotten."

## You Can Still Win The Race!

It's like the guy who took a wrong turn and still managed to win the 1995 New York City Marathon, a 26-mile run through the streets of the city.  A Mexican marathoner named German Silva and his teammate were leading the pack with about a mile to go when Silva took a wrong turn down a side street.

He ran a couple hundred yards in the wrong direction before realizing his mistake.  He reversed path, got back on the right road and overtook the leader to win by only two seconds!

What about you...which road are you headed down?  The job road?...Or the road to independence through free enterprise?

If you're on the job road, don't despair!  It's never too late to reverse your path and get back on the road to independence — the road I call *"the intelligent alternative."*

# PART 3

# An Intelligent Alternative:
# Independence Through Free Enterprise

# 9

---

## Own...Or Be Owned!

*The business of America is business.*
— Calvin Coolidge

Whenever I hear people griping and moaning about their jobs or the state of the economy, I'm always reminded of a great story about George, the forgetful salesman.

George was so absent-minded that he became the butt of daily office jokes. Not a day went by that someone in the office wouldn't yell down the hall, "George, you'd forget your head if it wasn't attached to your shoulders!"

One day as a late-morning department meeting was about to start, the sales manager pulled George aside and asked him to take his lunch break early so he could pick up sandwiches for the rest of the staff. As George was heading out the door, the manager turned to his staff and asked in mock seriousness, "Anybody in this room who's on a diet, please raise your hand."

About half the people in the room shot up their

hands. "Good," smirked the manager. "All you dieters will be happy to hear that I just asked George to pick up some sandwiches on his way back from lunch. I'll bet a month's wages he'll forget 'em!" The room erupted into laughter as everybody nodded knowingly.

An hour or so later George burst into the meeting room, red-faced and out of breath.

"You'll never guess what happened," he announced breathlessly to the startled group. "At lunch I ran into an old college buddy who's now president of a multi-billion dollar company," he gasped. "Well, we got to talking, and before I left, he ordered $15 million dollars worth of our products!"

The entire room burst into spontaneous applause at George's sudden success — except for the sales manager. The manager quickly quieted the celebration with a wave of his hand.

"Anything else you have to share with us, George?" asked the manager in a stern voice.

Startled by the question, George stammered, "No...was there something else?"

The sales manager frowned and threw his arms open wide in exasperation as he groaned, "See, I knew he'd forget the sandwiches."

## Keep Your Eye On The Big Picture

The moral of the story is that we need to stop majoring in the minor things! We need to *put things into proper perspective* by continually reminding ourselves of what the big picture really is.

The big picture for George's company was to sell products, which he did with a bang! But the manager couldn't see the forest for the trees. He was so focused on the tree right in front of him — George's forgetfulness — that he lost sight of the forest — making a profit.

The same can be said for so many people. Most of us get so locked into a job-mentality and so focused on the daily grind that we lose sight of the big picture — the endless opportunities that free enterprise offers.

## Putting Free Enterprise Into Perspective

Let's take a moment to put free enterprise into perspective by comparing it to the two other dominant economic systems of this century — socialism and communism. I first heard these common-sense definitions in a high school history class. The definitions were so simple to understand I remember them to this day:

COMMUNISM: You own two cows. The government takes both and gives you part of the milk.

SOCIALISM: You own two cows. The government takes one and gives it to your neighbor.

CAPITALISM: You own two cows. You sell one and buy a bull.

Pretty well sums it up, doesn't it? Given the three

systems, aren't you glad you're living and working in the one where you can "sell a cow and buy a bull"?

Or are you? I firmly believe that unless you own your own business, you're not really a full-fledged capitalist because you're not taking full advantage of the promise of free enterprise. Fact is, if you're working for someone else, you're participating in a different economic system I call "*Job-ism*."

Here's how I define it:

**JOB-ISM:** Your employer owns two cows. He pays you a dime to milk the cows and sells the milk for a dollar. He keeps both cows and all the profits.

This definition of job-ism illustrates the big difference between an employer and an employee. You see, the employer buys his employees at wholesale by paying them to do what he doesn't want to do. Then the employer sells their time and efforts at retail to the end consumer, pocketing the difference.

Look like a stacked deck to you? Then why are so many bright, able-bodied people willing — even eager — to settle for job-ism when they could take advantage of capitalism?

The best answer I can come up with is what I call the Oxygen Theory.

## Free Enterprise Is Like Oxygen

The Oxygen Theory goes like this: Living and working in the free enterprise system is like breathing oxygen. Oxygen is all around us from the day we take our very first breath. We breathe in, breathe out, without giving it a second thought. Oxygen is so plentiful that we take it for granted.

When was the last time you sat down and thanked God for the ability to breathe? Probably not since you were a kid and got held underwater by the neighborhood bully at the municipal pool.

We get so caught up in our lives, we start taking the things that are most dear to us for granted. Like oxygen. But what happens to people who develop emphysema? All of a sudden, they appreciate the miracle of breathing, and they savor every precious lungful of oxygen.

I believe the same can be said for free enterprise. If it didn't surround us, everybody would be clamoring for it. That's why immigrants from all over the world dream about coming to America, the "land of opportunity." They've been desperate for oxygen all their lives, and they keep hearing about a country where virtually anyone can gulp down all the oxygen he wants just by making the effort. Like oxygen, you must stop taking free enterprise for granted.

## Are You Driving The Train Or Riding In The Caboose?

I recently saw a full-page advertisement by Microsoft in the *Wall Street Journal* that eloquently explained the impact free enterprise has on all of our lives:

89

> *Business is the engine of society.*
> *Without it, there would be no jobs.*
> *No products.*
> *No competition.*
> *No advancements.*

Free enterprise is the engine, no doubt about it. Everything else is just along for the ride...including your job! That's why I call free enterprise "the intelligent alternative." Compared to communism, socialism and job-ism, free enterprise isn't just an intelligent alternative — it's the *only alternative!*

Free enterprise doesn't give a hoot about job security or corporate politics. Those are human concerns, not market forces. All free enterprise asks is that you identify a need and then fill it with a product or service that people are willing to pay a fair market price for.

## Trends Are Like Horses

It's easy to forget that just a few short years ago, communism was a very real threat to the free enterprise system. Today, the whole world is jumping on board the free enterprise train.

Make no mistake about it...*the dominant megatrend re-shaping the world today is free enterprise.* John Naisbitt, author of the best-seller *Mega-Trends*, summed up the importance of trends: "Trends are like horses," Naisbitt wrote. "It's easier to ride them in the direction they are going."

If the trend toward free enterprise is galloping down the straightaway, headed for the wire, why are so many Americans betting on the job market to win them financial independence?

I think it boils down to one word. *Dependence.*

# Independence: The Road Less Traveled

You know, I never have liked the word "dependence." After I looked the word up in my thesaurus, I liked it even less. Check out these synonyms:

DEPENDENCE: *Reliant. Subordinate. Secondary. Under. Controlled.*

The list went on for half a column. But there was only one antonym listed: *Independence.* Which tells me that you're either one...or the other.

A recent survey asked small business owners to list the best thing they liked about owning their own business. Know what 75 percent answered? *Independence.* More than money, more than time, more than anything I can think of, people want independence!

People want to come and go as they choose...people want to make their own decisions...and people DO NOT want to answer to anyone but themselves!

Think about it! This is the country that was founded by a *Declaration of Independence*...This is the country that built an *Independence Hall*...named a town *Independence, Missouri*...and celebrates *Independence Day.* We admire independent thinkers and people of independent means.

I mean, folks, *independence is the cornerstone of this country*.

If you're dependent on someone, whether it's **a**

parent or a boss, you're not totally free, isn't that true? You know, when I was a kid living at home, I had a pretty good deal. Room and board free. No expenses, to speak of. I had it made.

Only one problem. My parents were in control. They told me when to get up and when to come home. I lived by their rules, not mine. In exchange, I got three meals and a roof over my head for going along with the program, but I had to give up my freedom to get it. Sound like your job description?

Now, I don't know about you, but when I got to be 18 or so, I couldn't wait to make my own rules...to set my own hours...to get my own place...to be *independent!* As long as I was dependent on them, I had to do what they said or I faced the consequences. Their consequences.

I felt the same way after I worked at my first job for a while. At first, it was great. Then I started to resent answering to someone else in exchange for a small paycheck and a lot of unhappiness. Clocking in. Clocking out. Following rules, whether they made good sense or not. It was like living at home. *And I couldn't wait to move out!*

## Becoming Independent In A Job-Dependent World

It used to be that dependence was a stage that people went through while they were growing up. Unfortunately, today, for too many adults, dependence has become a way of life.

The worst part of dependence is that people get addicted to it...they get caught up in the comfort zone of their dependence and, more often than not, they stay there. Dependency is like being addicted to cigarettes. Once you're hooked, it's very difficult to become independent of them. Believe me, I know. I smoked cigarettes for 10 years...until the day of my 30th birthday when I asked myself this question: "Would I be better off at age 50 a smoker or a non-smoker?" I answered the question by throwing my last pack of cigarettes into the trash, never to touch them again.

Another example of dependence is welfare. This country has literally millions of healthy, able-bodied adults who are dependent on the U.S. taxpayers for their monthly checks. In time, they become comfortable with their dependence, justifying in their minds why they deserve it. Before they know it, they're addicted!

In his fascinating book *For Entrepreneurs Only*, Wilson Harrell sums it all up.

> *"Hear me now. Money is not what entrepreneurship is all about. Nor is power or influence. Those are nothing but measures of success. Let me tell you what an entrepreneur is all about. It's just one word. Such a simple word.* **Freedom!** *Freedom to get your head above the crowd. Freedom to be your own person. Freedom to have an idea, and to turn that idea into a business, and that business into an empire, if you can."*

When you examine the lives of most successful entrepreneurs, like Andrew Carnegie, you'll find their true motivation goes beyond money. Their true motivation is freedom and independence. They want to own, not be owned.

When Carnegie was a young man, for example, he was being groomed to take over as president of the Pennsylvania Railroad during a time when railroads were making money faster than the U.S. government could print it. He could have stayed at the railroad and become a multi-millionaire — not bad for the son of a poor Scottish immigrant.

But Carnegie resigned from his job at 30 to start his own business. In 1873 he founded U.S. Steel and then sold it in 1901 for $250 million. Now, that's a lot of money today. But back then the dollar was worth 100 times what it is today — plus there was no income tax! That same money today would be worth many billions of dollars!

Carnegie believed people should spend the first half of their lives creating wealth...and the second half giving it away to good causes. But he was also a seasoned businessman and a wise student of human nature. He knew better than to make people dependent upon his money.

That's why he put in safeguards to his contributions to ensure that the people who received his money didn't become dependent on it. For example, Carnegie set aside $60 million to build libraries in small towns all over the country. As many as 4,000 libraries were built from Carnegie's trust.

Carnegie insisted that each town come up with its

own money to buy the books, pay the staff and run the operation. That way they would remain independent, thus strong and viable for years after his death.

Carnegie's plan worked to perfection, proving once again the universal wisdom of the old adage: "If you give a man a fish, you feed him for a day. But if you teach a man to fish, you feed him for a lifetime."

To this day thousands of Carnegie libraries are still operating in the U.S., providing millions of people with virtually free access to history, literature and knowledge.

Wouldn't it be great to become a multi-millionaire, like Andrew Carnegie, and pass your final years giving away your fortune to those less fortunate than you? Only one small problem: Before you can give your fortune away, you have to create it first!

That's what the next chapter is about — the one enduring secret behind every great fortune that's ever been made...the secret that could empower you to become the next Andrew Carnegie.

# *10*

## So, What's The Secret Of The Wealthy, Anyway?

*"I don't want to be a millionaire. I just want to live like one."*
— Toots Shore, famous New York restaurant owner

A young newspaper reporter once asked Mark Twain, the great American novelist and humorist, his opinion of rich people.

"I'm opposed to millionaires. You can write that down," Twain bellowed. The young man nodded in agreement and scribbled furtively in his notebook as the great Twain took a long drag on his ever-present cigar.

Suddenly, Twain leaned forward in his rocking chair, removed the cigar from his mouth and whispered to the rookie reporter, "But it would be dangerous to offer me the position."

Twain's wry comment sums up America's love-hate relationship with the wealthy. We love to criticize wealthy people...but secretly we long to be wealthy ourselves.

Personally, I've never made any apologies for

wanting to be wealthy. When you grow up seeing poverty firsthand and what it does to people, you don't want any part of it, that's for sure.

The great English poet Lord Byron gave the best description I've ever heard of the power of money. He said, "Money is Aladdin's lamp." It's true! If you have enough money, you can get just about anything you wish for.

Just imagine for a minute that you were wealthy. What would you wish for?

A dream home and new cars for you and your spouse?

A top-notch education for your kids?

Longer vacations at first-class resorts around the world?

Or maybe you're the kind of person who would love to give something back, like Andrew Carnegie.

When you get right down to it, the issue isn't whether or not people want to be wealthy. In our heart of hearts, we all want to be wealthy. The reason more of us aren't wealthy is because we don't have a clue as to how to go about it!

## Own A Piece Of The Rock

*So what do rich people do to create wealth, anyway?*

The answer is a thousand different things. A few are professionals, like doctors, accountants or attorneys. Others have made a killing in insurance...Wall Street...real estate...franchising...distribution. The list goes on and on.

But America's wealthiest people all share one thing

in common, without exception. *They own.* They understand the pride and profit of ownership. If you own your own home, you know exactly what I mean!

The wealthiest Americans may own real estate... they may own stocks and bonds...they may own a business or two...they may own all of the above. Here's the kicker: *What* they own isn't really the key to creating wealth.

*The key to creating wealth is the principle of ownership itself!*

Here's a classic story that illustrates just what I mean. In 1960 a 20-year-old college dropout named Wayne took a job working on a garbage truck. Talk about a dead-end job! But instead of seeing a low-status, *low-paying job*, Wayne saw a *wealth-creating opportunity*. He learned the business...worked his way up to manager...saved his money...and then bought his own garbage truck.

Soon Wayne started buying up small local garbage hauling companies...then companies in nearby cities...then companies in cities all across America. Ten years later Wayne was part owner in Waste Management, the largest business of its kind in the world, earning over $2 billion in annual revenues!

In 1986 Wayne saw another opportunity in the emerging market of video rentals. He bought into a small chain of video stores named Blockbuster Video. Seven years later the original three Blockbuster stores had grown to 4,500 stores in 10 countries. Today Wayne is the owner of three professional sports teams in the Miami area, including the Miami Dolphins football team!

As you may have guessed, Wayne's last name is Huizenga, and it's a safe bet he's worth hundreds of millions of dollars. Now I ask you, if Huizenga had spent his life looking for better jobs instead of looking for better opportunities, do you think he would have created the wealth he has today? You and I both know the answer to that!

Look folks, the principle of ownership is so simple...so obvious...and so fundamental to creating wealth that I'm amazed every working person in this country isn't taking advantage of it!

Just look around. Who makes the money — the landlord or the tenant? Who's better off? The consumer who saves money by shopping at Wal-Mart?...or the person who owns shares of Wal-Mart stock? Who travels first-class? The guy who owns the automobile dealership...or the mechanic who works there?

## The Cornerstone Of The Free Enterprise System

If you don't see the big picture yet, check this out: Know what the single biggest asset is for most Americans? Their home, that's what. For example, let's say your parents bought a nice home in a nice neighborhood for $20,000 in 1960. Chances are they could sell it today for 10 times what they paid for it. Somebody writes mom and dad a check for $200,000 and they hit the road in a brand new RV and tuck the rest away in the bank. That's the difference between renting and owning.

Now, let's say over the years your parents had bought 10 nice homes located in nice neighborhoods. And 20 or so years later they sell them all. Good chance they'll see the world from the deck of a cruise ship...and still have enough left over to bank a cool million. That's the power of free enterprise!

Look, free enterprise isn't just about real estate.

*It's about the universal concept of ownership, the cornerstone of the free enterprise system.* It's up to you to choose the vehicle. Just make sure you have a stake in the equity, that's all I'm saying.

## What You Can Learn From The Rich

Last count, there were *over a million millionaires in the United States.* That calculates to be one millionaire for every 260 men, women and children in this country! Now, I don't believe that every one of those millionaires is smarter or more talented than you or I. You gotta figure a bunch of them are about average.

So what strategies are these "average" millionaires using to accumulate so much money? Doesn't it stand to reason that if you know what the millionaires with average talents and abilities are doing to get rich, you can copy them and get rich yourself?

A recent survey of over 165 millionaires gives us some insight into the secret of the top 1 percent of the wealthiest people in this country:

1. Only 10 percent inherited their money.

2. Almost 75 percent became rich by owning their own businesses.

3. The rich save and invest over 25 percent of their income.

This survey proves what I've been saying all along — *owning your own business offers you the best shot at creating wealth.* And the best way to stay rich is to buy ownership in other successful companies by saving and investing.

It's been right here in front of us the whole time. There's an abundance of opportunity available through free enterprise — especially now, more than ever!

Instead of looking for a job, you have to start looking for an opportunity. Instead of being *dependent* on the generosity of your employer, you must become *independent* by owning your own business.

According to futurist Edith Weiner, over 50 percent of the population will become entrepreneurs at the turn of the century, as affordable technology enables small companies to conduct business in ways that previously only big companies with big budgets could do.

Just imagine. One out of every two people in this country working for themselves! Already many Americans who are feeling shut out or held down by corporate America — namely laid-off workers, women and minorities — are jumping on the free enterprise bandwagon in a big way.

For example, the number of minority-owned businesses has doubled since 1982...and they're enjoying record profits. An estimated 6.5 million women own businesses, and experts predict that by the turn of the century, half of all small businesses — 15 million or more — will be owned by women.

• Men or women...black or white...old or young...what's the difference? There's more than enough to go around if we open our eyes to opportunity. Want proof? Check out what happened to some average people who made their fortunes by looking for — and finding — an opportunity:

• Jim Reid dove into a water hazard at a Florida golf course one day and came out with 2,000 golf balls. He quit his $250-a-week job at Walt Disney World and started a million-dollar company that recovers, washes and sells used golf balls.

• Rick Clunn was a bored systems analyst at Exxon who turned his passion for fishing into a full-time occupation. He won $1.5 million in prize money on the pro fishing tour, and earned hundreds of thousands more selling books and videos and holding fishing seminars.

• Kevin Eastman and Peter Laird made millions from doodles of four cartoon reptiles that turned into the Teenage Mutant Ninja Turtles.

• Bob Chandler became a millionaire after putting oversized tires on a truck and running over old cars at truck and automobile shows across the country.

• Gary Calvert figured out that Chestnut, Illinois, is the geographical center of the state. So he turned the small town into a tourist attraction. He makes a small fortune selling T-shirts, bumper stickers, pins, mugs and caps to free-spending tourists.

• Dave Hood had a friend videotape him driving bulldozers and earth movers at his job so he could show his kids what he did at work. Sure enough, every kid in the neighborhood wanted a copy. Today Dave is the star of seven different videos that gross millions of dollars annually.

## What's The Ideal Business For The First-Time Entrepreneur?

There are thousands and thousands of more stories just as fascinating as these. So what's the common denominator? It's turning opportunity into ownership.

There's no question about it, opportunity is abundant and available in this country. In fact, it's so abundant we're always tripping over it 'cause we're not looking for it.

Technology is opening up opportunities just about everywhere you look — entertainment, education, health care, personal growth, distribution, financial services, and on and on.

My most recent venture is a company called Equibore of America, Inc. We specialize in the installation of underground utilities, like fiber optics and telecommunications. Because of the information explosion and the demand to restore outdated utilities, the company's potential is mind-boggling.

But let's face it, not everybody has a quarter-million dollars in cash to invest in a new business and the wherewithal to leverage another half a million to start a new business, like I did with Equibore. Heck, most people can't write a check for $5,000, much less 100 times that much.

I'll be the first to remind you that it wasn't that long ago that I couldn't write a check for $500! But I've learned over the years that if you really, *really* want to start a business, you'll find the money somewhere, somehow. In fact, the lack of money is the poorest excuse for not starting a business.

Buying a home is a perfect example. Let's say you want to buy a $100,000 house. If you don't have the cash, does that mean you can't buy it? Of course not. You get a mortgage or a loan, don't you?

Same thing goes for starting your own business.

If you're really committed to independence, the question isn't whether or not you have enough money to start a business. The only question is, "What business should I get started in?"

How to answer that question is what the next chapter is all about.

# *11*

---

# The Ideal Business

*The system is the solution.*
—AT&T advertisement

*Buzz...Buzz...Buzz....*
For the last two hours, a housefly has been hurling his body against my office window, trying desperately to escape through the glass to freedom.
*Buzz...Buzz...Buzz....*
Not three feet from the glass pane is an open window. If the fly were to back away from the glass pane and head straight for the open window, he'd be free in a matter of seconds.
*Buzz...Buzz...Buzz....*
But he doesn't...and in the morning I'll find him on the same window sill, dead from exhaustion.

## Working Smarter, Not Harder

The fly is working very hard to achieve his dream of freedom, no doubt about it. But the sad truth is, no matter how hard he works, his strategy is doomed to failure. If the fly were more intelligent, he would soon realize he could accomplish his dream by working smarter instead of harder.

Fortunately, we're much smarter than flies ....

Or are we?

When it comes to work, most Americans are more like the fly than they care to admit. Did you know that today the average worker puts in nearly three more weeks at the office per year than workers did 25 years ago? Truth is, the 40-hour week has gradually turned into the 50-hour...even 60-hour week. When you factor in the increased cost of living (and increased payroll taxes), most Americans are working harder and taking home less!

If you're beginning to feel like a fly buzzing against a window pane, you aren't alone. As I see it, you've got two choices. You can keep working harder, beating yourself to death against that invisible wall called a job.

Or you can work smarter by backing away from that transparent wall and flying through the open window of free enterprise.

## The Ideal Business

Let's say you buy my argument that the only way to more freedom and independence...more happiness...and yes, more money...is to become an entrepreneur and own your own business. Let's say you're ready to begin your flight to freedom.

You could be sayin' to yourself, *O.K., Burke, I'm*

*with you. I believe you're 100 percent on the money. I'm totally sold! I'm ready to take advantage of free enterprise for myself and I'm ready right now! Only one question:*

*What business should I go into?*

Good question. In my opinion the ideal business isn't so much a business as it is *a system.* Let me explain:

Why is it that the local McDonald's restaurant — despite selling just OK hamburgers — makes zillions while Mom and Pop's Restaurant down the street — serving the best burger in town — is forced to close its doors?

More often than not, the difference is the system. Mom and Pop may be great cooks, but if they don't implement a successful plan...if they're disorganized...if they don't know how to market, they're destined for failure.

McDonald's, on the other hand, leaves nothing to chance. You order a Big Mac in Peoria, Illinois...or Peking, China...what happens? You're greeted with quick, friendly service, you get your burger in two minutes and it tastes just like every other Big Mac you've ever had. McDonald's proven success system is goof-proof. That's why virtually every franchise in their history makes a profit!

As the CEO of a major Fortune 500 company once remarked to a group of shareholders, "I'd reluctantly pay $1 for a great idea. But I'd gladly pay $1 million for the plan to implement that idea." That's why setting up a McDonald's franchise costs over a million bucks today. You're buying a proven system.

## Setting Up Your System

As I see it, you've got two choices when it comes to setting up a success system. You can either create your own...or you can follow one that's already been created. First, let's talk about how you go about creating your own success system:

Most likely you're good at what you do for a living. Fact is, you've developed a system in your job. Each day you perform a series of daily routines, which in turn make up your long-term success system — much like a series of small battles makes up a big war.

Before long you start thinking, *Hey, my boss is paying me $2,000 a month to do what I do. I know he's selling my services for five, maybe 10 times that much. Why should I make peanuts while he makes out like a bandit on my efforts?*

I like the way you're thinkin'! That's exactly how I got started in my first business. When I was 24 years old, I started selling cellular phones. It didn't take long to develop a system that enabled me to sell more phones than anyone else in the company. I figured that by opening my own operation, I could teach others my success system and make a percentage of their sales.

And that's exactly what I did.

Like many people, I had some basic skills and developed a *competence* by working for someone else. In turn, that competence gave me the *confidence* and experience to create a success system...and then take that system to go on my own.

I think it's safe to assume that many people who

start their own businesses do exactly what I did. They open their own business doing something they're good at and familiar with.

## Following In The Footsteps Of Franchisers

But what about the people who are good at what they do...but hate what they're doing? Think of all the people working for the government who fall into this category. Many government employees have tremendous talents, but those talents are being wasted in unfulfilling jobs. (If you work for the government, you know what I mean!)

It's imperative that you like what you do for a living. To paraphrase Will Rogers, "If you love what you do for a living, you never have to work another day as long as you live."

It wouldn't make sense, for example, for a great bookkeeper who hates bookkeeping to transfer her success system into opening her own bookkeeping business, would it? That would be like jumping from the frying pan into the fire!

## So, What Are Your Options?

My advice is to find a business you like that has a ready-made system you can follow. That way you reduce the chance of making costly mistakes. That's the beauty of buying into a franchise. I've known people who have invested in franchised restaurants, hotels, golf shops — you name it — and built them into high-profit businesses.

Sure, they did their homework before taking the leap. And it wasn't always easy. But eventually they learned the new system, worked hard and are now happily calling their own shots! No question about it...for most people, buying into a franchised success system is a lot safer than making up their own system.

The proof is in the pudding. It was just a short time ago, in the early 1960s, when the relatively new concept of franchising really caught on. Today franchising has grown into a $700-billion-a-year business. Experts estimate that today as much as one third of the goods and services in the country are moved through franchises.

What does this tell us about the awesome power of a duplicatable success system, like franchising? It works!

## Basic Ingredients To Success

As I see it, you need two basic ingredients to run a successful franchise: financial resources and specialized skills. In short, you've got to have enough money to set up the franchise. And you've got to have the skills to make it work. The key to becoming wealthy with franchises is to own several of them. Just ask any franchise owner.

When I first started looking at going into business for myself, I had little money...so traditional franchising wasn't a realistic alternative for me (just as buying into a franchise is not a realistic alternative for most people because they simply don't have enough money).

However, as I was closing the doors on my first business, I learned about a fast-growing franchising concept I call "the Alternative Franchise,"™ better known as network marketing.

## The Alternative Franchise™

I call network marketing the Alternative Franchise because it has all the great advantages of a franchise without the incredibly high startup costs of most proven franchises. You can get started in an Alternative Franchise for less than $500 — with the upside potential of leveraging your business into a multi-million-dollar-a-year enterprise!

As for the need to have specialized skills in order to succeed, that's the beauty of it, because the established and proven networking companies — like successful franchises — have a duplicatable system in place for you to learn and follow.

If you have a willingness to work, a burning desire to succeed and you're coachable, you can literally start making a profit from day one...while you are still learning the ins and outs of the business!

Furthermore, what I find most valuable about this industry is that it can offer you the equivalent of a Harvard-type education in personal growth while you build your business.

In my opinion, the Alternative Franchise is the single best system available today, particularly for the first-time entrepreneur...or for the seasoned entrepreneur who wants a ready-made system to follow and work. You can start part-time...the up-front costs are ridiculously low compared to traditional businesses...and you have easy access to top-notch training and mentorship from the most successful people in the industry!

Again, in my opinion, the Alternative Franchise is the single best system available today with the potential to earn a fortune without having to invest a fortune. It's a no-brainer!

## Why The Awesome Growth?

According to the Direct Sales Association, the Alternative Franchise is over a $10-billion-a-year business. That's 10,000 million bucks, amigos...and growing! That's bigger than Hollywood!

I believe that's just the tip of the iceberg! Given the dynamic growth rate in both domestic and foreign markets — coupled with a global shift in the way people think and work — I predict the Alternative Franchise will become a $100-billion-per-year industry in the next 10 to 15 years!

That's $90 billion in new business, folks! And who do you think will get the lion's share of that new business? The stable, mature companies with proven track records and their distributors, that's who!

Why the awesome growth? Two basic reasons: Number one, technology is finally affordable and available to the average person. For example, you can set up a home office complete with a fax machine, computer, cellular phone, voice mail and on and on for a fraction of what it would have cost 10 years ago.

And two, networking, unlike conventional businesses, takes full advantage of a simple yet dynamic concept we first learned about back in third grade — *multiplication*. Let's take a look at how the concept of multiplication can lead to exponential growth:

## The Power Of Multiplication

Let's say you work your networking business part-time, 10 hours per week. Let's also say you recruited 10 like-minded associates to join you in your business, each also working 10 hours a week.

Look at what has happened here: Through the power of multiplication, you're now able to get paid on 110 hours of effort: 10 x 10 = 100 hours per week that your associates are working...plus your 10 hours! Compare that to a typical 40-hour work week!

It's no wonder the concept of multiplication — also known as "compounding" and "leveraging" — is the basic concept behind the world's great fortunes.

Now, here's the kicker.

Imagine over time you had 100 people in your business, all working only 10 hours a week. You could be earning profits from *1,000 hours worth of effort each and every week!*

That's why it's not uncommon for laid-off factory workers...ex-school teachers...former executives — even disillusioned doctors and lawyers — to build organizations numbering in the thousands — even tens of thousands!

No wonder some experienced distributors live lifestyles of the rich and famous...without ever having to answer to a boss again as long as they live!

## What Do You Do When Opportunity Knocks?

Look, it's not my position to choose a business for you. However, I do feel obligated to make you aware of what's out there so you can make an intelligent, informed choice.

If you want to learn more about the concept of the Alternative Franchise, I suggest you pick up a copy of my first book, *Who Stole The American Dream?*, which discusses the industry in detail.

Maybe the Alternative Franchise is for you — or maybe it's not. One thing's for sure. You won't know until you check it out, will you? I always say a wise man investigates what a fool takes for granted — so check it out!

There's an old vaudeville routine that always comes to mind when I talk to people about opportunity. Two old comics are in the middle of their song-and-dance routine, when one says to the other: "When opportunity knocks, you gotta open the door."

His partner looks over at him, shrugs and wise-cracks, "Yeah, opportunity knocked on your door once. But by the time you turned off the burglar alarm, removed the safety bar, loosened the guard chain and unlocked the dead bolt, it was gone."

True, "better safe than sorry" is good advice.

But "better successful than safe" is the best advice of all.

116

# 12

## You Can't Steal Second With Your Foot On First!

*I already made up my mind. I just made it up both ways.*
— Casey Stengel

In 1955, the founder and president of a struggling young Japanese company invented the world's first transistor radio. A huge American watch company, Bulova, was so impressed they offered to buy 100,000 transistor radios and resell them under the Bulova name.

Now, what would you have done if you were president of that small, struggling company? *Would you have played it safe* and made the sale, knowing that Bulova would probably order millions more radios in the coming years?

*Or would you have said to yourself, "better successful than safe"* and turned down Bulova's offer, electing instead to take a calculated risk in order to make a bigger profit (and a bigger name for yourself) by selling the radios under your company's name?

If you were Akio Morita, you'd have taken the risk

...and it would have paid off bigger than anyone could have predicted! Your company would have become a household name by manufacturing and marketing affordable, innovative electronic products, like the first transistor radios, the first VCRs and the first CD players.

Today that once obscure little Japanese company generates $35 billion a year in revenues and has far surpassed Bulova in annual earnings.... And far surpassed every competitor as a name consumers recognize and trust — Sony.

## No Guts, No Glory

When the stunned manager from Bulova asked Morita why he turned down their order, he replied, "I am now taking the first step for the next 50 years for my company."

You see, Morita had a big vision that required him to take a calculated risk. He wanted the *independence* to make Sony the biggest and best electronics company in history, and he was well aware he couldn't do that riding the shirttails of Bulova. If he did the deal with Bulova, he'd always be *dependent* on them. For Morita, dependence wasn't even an option.

Because Morita took a calculated risk, he not only made big money...he made history. Before Sony, Japan was known for producing cheap stuff that broke easily. When you described something as being "made in Japan," you were making a joke...calling it junk.

Sony changed all that. Today "made in Japan" is

synonymous with quality.

No wonder Morita is a national hero in Japan!

## Everything's A Risk

Like I said in the first part of this book, no matter what you do, there is always risk.

You go for a walk, you risk getting hit by a car.

You get married, you risk getting a divorce.

You opt for the security of a job, you risk getting laid off.

A poem one of my business partners faxed me the other day says it best.

It's called *Risking.*

> *To laugh is to risk appearing a fool.*
>
> *To weep is to risk appearing sentimental.*
>
> *To love is to risk not being loved in return.*
>
> *To live is to risk dying.*
>
> *To hope is to risk despair.*
>
> *To try is to risk failure.*
>
> *But risks must be taken because the greatest hazard in life is to risk nothing.*
>
> *The person who risks nothing, does nothing, has nothing, is nothing.*
>
> *He may avoid suffering and sorrow, but he simply cannot learn, feel, change, grow, love, live.*
>
> *Chained by his own fears, he is a slave. He has forfeited freedom.*
>
> *Only a person who risks is free!*

119

## We Can't Have It Both Ways

*Only the person who risks is free!*
That last line is oh, so powerful...and oh, so true. If you think about it, that's what this country's about. That's really what capitalism and a free market society are all about. This country's about the opportunity — not the *right* — to become independent.

Free enterprise is NOT the right to be protected from failure.

Free enterprise is NOT the right to a free lunch.

Free enterprise is NOT the right to "do your own thing" without taking responsibility for the consequences!

Like I said earlier, *either way, you pay!*

Here's the catch. Seems like today, more than ever before, we want to have it both ways. We want security...but we want the big rewards that go along with calculated risks. In short, we want our cake but we want...no, make that *we demand to eat it, too*. And that's simply NOT POSSIBLE!

## There Is No Santa Claus

On one hand we want the government to play Santa Claus, handing out entitlements like "free" health insurance and generous social security payments and cushy government jobs like candy...on the other hand *we want lower taxes!*

On one hand we want the government to cut through all the red tape...eliminate those annoying regulations for business and industry...on the other hand *we want protection from failure with Washington's endless subsidies and entitlements!*

Hey, folks. It's time for a reality check. Here's a basic law of physics. Ready?

*For every force, there's an equal and opposite force.*

The Chinese call it the "yin and the yang":

*Life & death...*

*Old & young...*

*Light & dark...*

*Happy & sad...*

*Rich & poor...*

That's why you can't stuff your face with pizza, followed by a half-gallon of ice cream, at every meal, never exercise and realistically expect to lose weight.

And that's why you can't enjoy the freedom in free enterprise — freedom to set your own hours, be your own boss, make your own decisions, control your own destiny — while you're voluntarily chained to the "security" of a job.

## Get Off The Fence!

I want you to play a game of pretend with me, OK?

Pretend I just handed you a big red balloon. Now pretend I'll give you a $1,000 bill if you can do one simple thing for me. Ready?

Place the open end of the balloon in your mouth. Take a deep breath.

OK, for $1,000, SUCK AND BLOW AT THE EXACT SAME TIME!

How'd you do? Not so good, eh? How about if I guaranteed you $2,000? $20,000? $2 million? Name your own figure .... You still can't inhale and exhale at the same time!

The same holds true for free enterprise, folks. You can't steal second with your foot on first. You can't be financially free unless you step out of your comfort zone and take a chance on you! You can't swim the English Channel with one foot on the shore. Wake up to the obvious, folks!

Now don't get me wrong. You can work part-time at an opportunity while holding down a full-time job, no question about it. But to be really free, at some point you have to let the job go! End of subject!

## Here Today, Gone Tomorrow

Look, if I sound like I'm a chest-thumping champion of free enterprise, you're right on! Let me share a story with you about a man named Osborne and perhaps you'll appreciate why I'm so sensitive about the subject — and why I'm so outspoken with my opinions.

As you read this story, perhaps you'll understand my passion for championing the incredible power of the free enterprise system. As I travel the country and the world giving speeches and seminars on free enterprise, what I communicate to people comes from a sincere and very personal perspective. And the more people I'm able to touch with my message, the greater my reward.

It was Christmas Day, 1958, and Osborne was on top of the world. According to *Time Magazine*, he was worth almost $20 million dollars. He had a beautiful young wife and a handsome two-year-old son. He lived in a mansion and owned five vacation homes. He had a chauffeured limousine at his command day and night.

Osborne owned many successful businesses and controlled vast holdings in real estate. He was recognized around the world as a leader in the textile industry, and his factories employed thousands of workers. He was even appointed Cuba's ambassador to Brazil.

Like I said, on top of the world.

Less than a month later, Osborne woke up one morning from a deep, peaceful sleep to discover he'd lost everything. No more money. No more servants. No more mansion. No more real estate. No more businesses. Everything he worked so hard for was gone forever.

Now, a lot of people who lost a lot less than Osborne jumped off tall buildings in the stock market crash of '29. But to Osborne's credit, he was down...but not out.

Osborne never recovered his vast fortune, but he did recover his dignity. And he did manage to fight his way back from being broke to running several successful businesses in the Caribbean and South America.

I knew Osborne personally, so I knew what he went through. How he suffered. How the anger and frustration ate away at his health. But self pity? Not a chance! In the face of outrageous misfortune...of the gravest injustice...Osborne never wallowed in self pity.

You see, Osborne was Burke Osborne Hedges, my father. He was one of the wealthiest men in Cuba before a power-hungry communist named Fidel Castro confiscated all of my father's companies...bank accounts...real estate...everything... for "crimes against the people."

Know what my father's crime was? His companies employed thousands of people throughout Cuba and Latin America in 1958. Today, the only "business" still in operation is a textile factory outside Havana, Cuba.

Perhaps now you understand why the free enterprise system is so dear to me. Nobody should have to go through what my father went through! That's why I've made it my life's mission to spread the message of free enterprise to as many people as possible so they don't take it for granted.

## Cherish And Cultivate Your Independence

Zig Ziglar, one of America's greatest sales and personal development trainers, once remarked that "Any government big enough to give you what you want is big enough to take it away." The businessmen and women who lost everything to Fidel Castro's Communist government know what Zig means. Big time!

The Cubans who were poor before Castro took over can fully appreciate Zig's words of wisdom, too. Today they're not only without money...and land. They're also without the most precious thing in the world — *freedom*. When Castro took over, he took it all...the "free" and the "enterprise."

The only thing Castro left is despair.

Fortunately, it's not too late for this country. Or even for Canada, where our friends to the north can tell us a thing or two about the perils of being dependent on Big Government for a job.

Free enterprise is like the right to vote. If you don't use it, you lose it. And I'm here to remind you that you must stake your claim on the virtue that made this country great — independence — by seizing the opportunities free enterprise offers each of us.

# 13

## Signing Your Personal Declaration Of Independence

*His brow is wet with honest sweat,*
*He earns whate'er he can.*
*And looks the whole world in the face,*
*For he owes not any man.*
— Henry Wadsworth Longfellow

Over 250 years ago 56 men met in a hot, muggy room in Philadelphia to create possibly the most profound document in history, with the obvious exception of the Bible.

They called the document the *Declaration of Independence.*

*The document wasn't very long* — about the equivalent of two or three typed pages today.

*It didn't require a lot of scholarly research* — Thomas Jefferson, the principle author, wrote it without notes, saying he just wanted to "place before mankind the common sense of the subject."

*The purpose of the document was clear and straightforward* — independence manifested through "an expression of the American mind," in Jefferson's words.

The document contained time-honored truths in

simple language, powerful life-altering truths that to this day continue to topple dictatorships and to free people all over the world.

Here's, perhaps, the most famous sentence in modern history:

> *We hold these truths to be self evident, that all men are created equal, that they are endowed by their Creator with certain unalienable Rights, that among these are Life, Liberty and the pursuit of Happiness.*

The Declaration of Independence says just about everything that needs to be said about freedom, a concept very near and dear to my heart.

## What Free Enterprise Is Not

If you want to know *what free enterprise is NOT*, just take a look at Cuba. Fidel Castro has appointed himself as the country's "daddy" and treats all Cuban citizens as if they were his children.

For over 35 years "daddy" has systematically and purposefully run the Cuban economy into the ground while making the Cuban people dependent on his government for virtually everything. Here's a look at what happens when you trade personal independence for dependence on the government:

Let's say you're a small peanut farmer in Cuba. You work and sweat all day to grow your small crop. In Cuba there is no fertilizer for your crops...no pesticide to fight the bugs...and no gasoline to run the tractor that tills the ground and harvests the crop. When the peanuts are ready for market, the first "market" you must sell to is the government, which pays 71 pesos for 100 pounds.

Those same peanuts would bring 2,000 pesos on the open market...almost 30 times what the government pays! Yet by law you are forced to sell your hard-earned crop to the government only.

Did you know that in Cuba you can be fined for failing to register a newborn calf? If you slaughter a pig or a cow, you can go to jail for eight years — even if it's a pig or cow you birthed, fed and raised!

Why? Because when you're dependent on the government, the government owns everything you possess — and you along with it!

This is what free enterprise is NOT!!

## Don't Take Anything For Granted

When I was 12, my father and I used to play chess together almost every weekend. One day as our game was coming to an end, my father said something I've never forgotten, something that's had a tremendous impact on my life.

With grave seriousness he looked directly into my eyes and said, *Burkie, don't ever take anything for granted.* I didn't know exactly what he meant at the time, but he said it with such utter conviction that his words were burned into my memory.

*Don't ever take anything for granted.*

Today, that message haunts me more than ever. I look around me and see this wonderful land of ours, full of promise and potential. And I see people taking for granted the very thing that this country was founded on — freedom.

*Freedom to think...say...do...become...just about anything.*

So what do we do with that freedom? We tuck it away in a safe place in the closet. We've replaced the true meaning of *freedom* — independence through personal responsibility and individual efforts — with *license,* which is the freedom to do what you want without regard to the consequences.

Look, we have this wonderful legacy of total freedom through free enterprise dropped in our laps, and what do we do? We insist on job security...government subsidies...cushy entitlements...I'll-sue-you-if-you-fire-me mentality...and on and on. *We run for cover, that's what we do.*

What happened to rugged individualism?

What happened to self-reliance?

What happened to Horatio Alger stories?

What happened to the dreams that spawned the gold rush...the call of "Westward, Ho"...the chorus of "Let freedom ring"? I'll tell you what happened. Most Americans have accepted mediocrity as a way of life...and sold their soul for a government pension.

## Follow Your Star

Look, I don't want you to think I'm anti-government. I'm pro-government! I'll be the first to tell you we need a system of government to effectively operate U.S.A., Inc. Can you imagine where we'd be without our government…without our military? We need soldiers, air force pilots, police officers, firefighters, zoning officials and the like. Flaws and all, our system of government is still the greatest in the world!

If you're currently working for the government, and you can look yourself in the mirror and honestly say, "This is my life's mission," then be proud. Keep on doing what you're doing because this country needs you, friend.

But if you're unhappy and unfulfilled as a civil servant (or a dissatisfied employee in the private sector), then I recommend you move on. There's a whole big world of opportunity just waiting for you…if you'll just take your foot off first.

## Your Declaration Of Independence

Those 56 brave men who signed the first Declaration of Independence had a lot to lose. One of the original signers, Ben Franklin, summed it up when asked what would happen if the signers became divided and the revolution failed: "We'll either all hang together, or we'll hang separately."

Talk about commitment. Talk about puttin' it all on the line. Just look at the last line of the Declaration of Independence:

> *And for support of this Declaration, with a firm reliance on the Protection of Divine Providence, we mutually pledge to each other our Lives, our Fortunes and our sacred Honor.*

Now, many of these men were well off financially. They were successful businessmen who either came from money or owned lots of land. They could have "sold out"...played it safe...and most likely would have done just fine managing their estates under the British crown.

But they risked "our Lives, our Fortunes and our sacred Honor" for freedom.

What about you? Are you truly free?

Free from the tyranny of a boss?

Free from office politics?

Free from board-room decisions that you have no control over?

Free from long hours?

Free from lack of money?

Ask yourself, "Am I truly free to realize my childhood dreams of making my own way in the world...calling my own shots...running my own show?"

If the answer is no, then it's time to stand up and be counted. It's time to sign your own Personal Declaration of Independence.

If you are truly sincere about kicking the American addiction of being broke...sincere about living the dream of owning your own business...sincere about realizing total freedom through free enterprise...sincere about pulling yourself out of the job rut...then you must sign your Personal Declaration of Independence right now!

I've drafted a copy for you. Find a pen (not a pencil). Now sign in ink (better yet, blood). Here goes.

# Personal Declaration Of Independence

*When in the course of human events, it becomes necessary for each person to dissolve the economic bonds that tie us to dead-end jobs and unwanted bosses, it behooves each of us to pursue excellence, personal fulfillment and financial independence through Free Enterprise.*

*I hold these truths to be self-evident, that Free Enterprise is not the private domain of any one gender, race or religion; furthermore, I fully recognize that I possess certain God-given talents and abilities, among them the ability to think, dream, learn, act and believe.*

*Let it be said, therefore, that from this day forth I choose of my own free will to realize my fullest potential by starting and running my own business.*

_____    _____

*Signed and Attested*                          *Date*

Congratulations! You've taken the first step to becoming independent in a job-dependent world. Your next step is to get started.

You've thought about owning your own business...you've dreamed about it...and now it's time to take action.

As a wise man once said, "Don't be afraid to take a big step if one is required. You can't leap across a canyon in two small jumps."

# *14*

## You Can't Judge A Book By Its Cover

*There is a tide in the affairs of men,*
*Which, taken at the flood, leads on to fortune;*
*Omitted, all the voyage of their life*
*Is bound in shallows and misery.*
— William Shakespeare

Several years ago I heard a very special story I've never forgotten. I believe this story captures the very essence of what I want this book to communicate to you.

Namely, that more often than not, what we want most in life is right in front of us if we're willing to just open our eyes and accept what we see.

The story is about a selfish, hot-tempered young man and his wealthy, deeply religious father. The young man's mother had died when he was a youngster. Afraid of spoiling his only child, the father was oftentimes overly strict with his hot-headed son.

The young man was about to graduate from college, and he and his father had often discussed what kind of graduation present the young man wanted. After much deliberation, the son decided he wanted an exotic sports car, a life-long dream. His father agreed that a new car would be a fitting present for such a special occasion.

On graduation day, the father and his best friend from childhood attended the graduation ceremonies. After the young man received his diploma, the proud father hugged him and, with tears in his eyes, told his son that this was the happiest day of his life. With that, the father handed his son a hastily wrapped package, saying, "I'm delighted to give you a present that, I pray, you will enjoy for the rest of your life."

The smiling boy tore the wrapping off his gift. But in a flash, his smile dissolved into a frown...then an angry scorn. Instead of the present he had dreamed about for so long — a set of shiny new car keys — the father had presented his son with a brand-new Bible.

Disappointment quickly turned into rage. The hot-headed young man looked at his father in disbelief. Holding the Bible in front like an offering, the dis-traught young man shouted, "How could you give me *this* when you knew I wanted a new car?"

He lifted the Bible high above his head and threw it down at his father's feet with all his might screaming, "This is what I think of your graduation gift. I hate it...and I hate you!"

Then he turned and ran from the auditorium as his father shouted after him, "Wait! You don't under-stand...It's not what you think!" The spoiled young man never heard his father's full explanation, for as he ran from the building, his father clutched his chest and fell to the ground, dead from a massive heart attack.

Years passed. Over time the son grew from a selfish,

hot-tempered young man into a kind, considerate middle-aged father with children of his own. One lovely spring morning he heard a faint knock on the door. There on the front porch was a bent old man holding a Bible in one hand and leaning on a cane with the other. The middle-aged man recognized the old man as his father's best friend, and immediately swung the door open wide, inviting him in.

They retired to the den and spent the rest of the morning reminiscing about the good old days. Before leaving, the old man turned gravely serious. He leaned forward in his chair and asked, "Do you know what's in this Bible?"

The younger man nodded and replied, "Why, yes I do. Not long after my father's death, I began a serious search to find the answer to the meaning of life. My search led me to all four corners of the earth...and to my eventual realization that there are no truer words than those written in the Bible."

The old man seemed pleased with the answer, knowing that his long-deceased father would be happy to know his only son found his faith. Then he turned away and looked out the window.

After a moment of silence he turned back and said, "I'm an old man, and I don't have long for this world. I want you to know I've debated long and hard over whether or not to pay this visit. But now that we've talked, I'm convinced I did the right thing. Your father would be proud!"

The younger man was visibly moved by the old man's compliment. And his eyes glistened in the sun-lit den.

"When I asked you if you knew what's in this Bible," the old man resumed, "I was delighted to hear of your conviction. But I wasn't speaking in the figurative sense. I meant what I said literally. Do you know what's in THIS BIBLE?"

As he spoke he extended his arm forward so that the Bible was only inches away from the younger man's face. "Well, I guess I don't," the younger man replied with confusion in his voice.

"This is the Bible your father gave you the day you graduated from college. I picked it up after your father collapsed, and I've kept it for all these years, waiting for the right time to present it to you. Now is that time.

"I'll leave this Bible with you," the old man continued. "And I trust you'll look through it carefully after I leave. I think you'll find something in here that may change your opinion of your father."

After escorting the old man to the front door, the younger man returned to his den, picked up the faded Bible and began thumbing slowly through the yellowed pages. As he turned the pages, he remembered his father's "betrayal" on graduation night, and he remembered the anger that consumed him so many years ago...until he turned the last page of the Bible to find...taped to the inside back cover...the tarnished keys to a new car.

The man paused for a moment, frozen in time. He sat in stunned silence, replaying in his mind the ugly scene that led to his father's fatal heart attack years ago. Then he began to cry.

## Perception vs. Reality

This story is a classic reminder that perception is reality — we see what we want to see and believe what we want to believe. If we want to perceive the truth, we have to look with an open mind and dig beneath the surface.

The young man in the story *perceived* what most of us in his situation would perceive — that the Bible couldn't possibly contain what he wanted most in the world — a new car. In *reality*, the Bible contained not only the key to his car, but the key to wisdom and eternal life.

Like the lesson in the story, there's a big difference between what most of us perceive and the reality of today's global marketplace.

*We perceive* that a job is the only way to security.

*We perceive* that going into business for yourself is too risky.

*We perceive* that the government (or a generous employer) will provide us with a safety net forever.

*We perceive* that other people were meant to own businesses, but not *me*.

*We perceive* that wealth and freedom are for someone else, but not *me*.

That's the perception. Here's the reality.

*The reality* is that the only guarantee in life is in your shoes.

*The reality* is that only you are in control of where you want to be in 10 years.

*The reality* is that depending on a job is the ultimate risk.

*The reality* is that lifetime employment is dead and gone forever.

*The reality* is that the government's lifetime safety net is so threadbare and full of holes that it will disintegrate when the baby-boomers start falling into it!

*The reality is the only way to become independent in a job-dependent world is to take a calculated risk and go into business for yourself!*

## Either Way, You Pay!

Friends, it's time to look into the mirror and ask yourself some tough questions:

How many times have you started a job with great expectations — only to find out after six months (or six years) that once again, you're unhappy and unfulfilled?

How many times do you have to get knocked in the head before you shout, "Stop the insanity!  I don't deserve this kind of treatment!  And I won't put up with it anymore!"?

Friends, you don't have to run in place on the job treadmill if you don't want to.  There are plenty of golden, glorious opportunities out there.  More opportunities than jobs if you will only open your eyes and look!

All the products have NOT been invented.

All the needs have NOT been met.

All the services have NOT been offered.

All the products have NOT been distributed.

What are you waiting for?  Someone is going to fill those needs.  Why not you?  Why not now?

I'm here to remind you that opportunities are never missed.  Someone else just takes advantage of them first.

Instead of making up excuses about why you CAN NOT go into business for yourself, you have to start looking for reasons why YOU CAN!

So what's the next step? It's obvious. If you're a dis-satisfied employee, right now — today — is the best time to take the initiative to find a business you would enjoy and could earn a profit from.

Please don't be like the immature, close-minded boy in the story.  He didn't take the initiative to look through the Bible his father gave him — and it cost him dearly!

Open your eyes to opportunity...open your mind to possibilities...and open your heart to the freedom available through free enterprise.

Go ahead...I challenge you.

Take your foot off first.

Make a run for second.

And never, never look back.